CREATING THE CUSTOMER-DRIVEN ACADEMIC LIBRARY

Jeannette Woodward

AMERICAN LIBRARY ASSOCIATION

Chicago   2009

JEANNETTE WOODWARD is a principal of Wind River Library and Nonprofit Consulting. After a career in academic library administration, she began a second career in public libraries, serving as director of the Fremont County Library System in the foothills of the Wind River Mountains of Wyoming. Woodward is the author of several books, including *What Every Librarian Should Know about Electronic Privacy* (2007), *Nonprofit Essentials: Managing Technology* (2006), *Creating the Customer-Driven Library: Building on the Bookstore Model* (2005), and *Countdown to a New Library: Managing the Building Project* (2000). She holds a master's degree in library and information science from Rutgers University, with doctoral study at the University of Texas at Austin.

The paper used in this publication meets the minimum requirements of American National Standard for Information Sciences—Permanence of Paper for Printed Library Materials, ANSI Z39.48-1992. ⊚

Library of Congress Cataloging-in-Publication Data

Woodward, Jeannette A.
Creating the customer-driven academic library / Jeannette Woodward.
    p.   cm.
Includes bibliographical references and index.
ISBN 978-0-8389-0976-8 (alk. paper)
1. Academic libraries—United States. 2. Public services (Libraries). 3. Academic libraries—Space utilization—Social aspects. 4. Academic libraries—Marketing. 5. Academic libraries—Public relations. I. Title.
Z675.U5W78 2009
027.70973—dc22

2008022360

ISBN-13: 978-0-8389-0976-8

Printed in the United States of America
13   12   11   10   09   5   4   3   2   1

To my family

Laura, Chris, Lowell, John, and Davey

with all my love

CONTENTS

Additional materials are available on the book's website,
at www.ala.org/editions/extras/woodward09768.

INTRODUCTION

The traditional academic library, the vast building staffed by reference librarians and circulation clerks, catalogers and collection development specialists, professionals, paraprofessionals, and legions of student workers, is going through what may be the most difficult period in its history.

With more and more scholarly materials available online and accessible from any personal computer, where does the academic library fit in? Change has come so rapidly that academic librarians can scarcely keep their heads above water. How must the library evolve if it is to remain relevant? How can librarians justify the vast investment in real estate these libraries require, and how does that real estate contribute to the library's mission?

RESPONDING TO CHANGING NEEDS

Academic librarians have done an amazing job of retooling both themselves and their libraries, developing new services as they identify new needs. However, they may still find themselves vainly marketing yesterday's library to students and faculty who prepare for class at a coffee shop or go home and curl up in a comfy chair with their personal laptop computers. How can the library compete with the comforts of home or the local Starbucks?

Librarians have repeatedly shown themselves able to respond to the changing needs of their customers. Yet, to some extent, they have not yet confronted the most troublesome challenge looming on the horizon. How will they transform and bring new life to libraries organized around the acres of printed materials that constitute yesterday's libraries? How can they ensure that academic libraries and librarians will still have a vital place in twenty-first-century academic life and will continue to have the resources to meet the information needs of the academic community? Surviving and prospering in this new century will require a total rethinking of the nature of the library and the role of academic librarians. This book will attempt to bring together the creative responses of a wide range of academic librarians, uncovering successful strategies and focusing on trailblazing approaches most likely to succeed in the challenging environment of the twenty-first-century academy.

From the birth of academic librarianship, our profession has modeled itself on the teaching faculty. Outnumbered and sometimes mistreated, we have sought to be considered full members of the faculty with all their rights and privileges. Such recognition has allowed us to participate more fully in the life of our academic institutions, given us a voice in curriculum development, and established our right to academic freedom. However, this has not come without a price.

Academic culture emphasizes cerebral pursuits, freedom from material concerns, and sometimes just plain grubbiness. Whether voluntarily or involuntarily, academic librarians have often followed along this same path. Because our libraries are resource-driven to a much greater extent than other types of libraries, we have been forced to scrimp on funding that impacts the look and feel (and smell) of our public spaces. In fact, our libraries sometimes look as dreary as the college classrooms that students find much too uncomfortable to visit voluntarily. In the 1960s some of the grubbiness was replaced by the sterile look of hospitals, and in the 1970s burnt orange, avocado, and harvest gold decor prevailed. Soon, both sterility and "mod" color schemes gave way to yet more squalor, but without the charm of traditional architecture. Many of these buildings have been replaced, but the new structures may still be meeting the needs of yesterday's library users.

THE SCOPE OF THIS BOOK

The academic libraries described in this book are made of bricks and mortar. Although digital libraries are among the most exciting recent developments, this book will focus on the more familiar and more traditional libraries that welcome freshmen for information literacy classes, dispense face-to-face reference assistance, and provide comfortable havens for weary students. With more and more scholarly materials available online and accessible from any desktop or laptop computer, what is the future role of the traditional academic library? How can it evolve to meet the needs of twenty-first-century students, and how must librarians themselves evolve to meet these needs?

To be very blunt, this book also focuses on survival, and to a large extent survival depends on the number of students and faculty who enter the library through doors made of wood or glass or stainless steel. This is not to say that the library's virtual presence on the World Wide Web is not important. The virtual library serves our customers in many important ways, but the academic community continues to view these efforts as separate and apart from "the library." There is evidence that some misguided administrators believe that library buildings are no longer needed and virtual libraries can completely replace them. They argue that negotiating for periodical databases and other online resources can be done by a clerk in the university business office acting on requests from academic departments. Although most college and university decision makers do not share this radical view, what they know of the library is what they see. When they enter a library that is filled with endless stack ranges but nearly empty of students, they see valuable real estate that could be better used.

The Customer Point of View

Having visited many academic libraries while writing this book, I have naturally included descriptions of some of the more exciting innovations I've encountered. However, I should say at the onset that this book is not just about innovative new spaces and services. Rather, I have tried to describe academic libraries as customers, usually students, see them. I have pieced together the comments and experiences of a large number of students, some of whom I've interviewed and others whom I've known over the course of my own library career. As you might expect, they view the library in a way that is very different from the way librarians view it, and they don't see the library in terms of innovative new services. What they know of the library is what they themselves encounter. When they praise or criticize the library, they're really talking about themselves and their own needs. In other words, they will notice the comfortable chair or unfriendly staff member, but probably fail to notice organizational changes unless those changes make a real difference in their experience.

Additionally, it must be emphasized that this book is not focused on the library's academic mission. Instead, it is directed at stabilizing and enhancing the underlying structure that makes it possible to pursue that mission. A library that is struggling for its very survival is unable to meet the academic needs of its community. Many ingredients are needed if one is to create a recipe for a successful academic library, but none is more essential than a core of satisfied customers who use the library themselves, encourage others to do the same, and spread the word that the library is alive and well in the twenty-first century.

Library 2.0

Throughout this book, you will find sections that discuss or mention in passing Library 2.0, the paradigm that is sweeping both public and academic libraries. I should make it clear that although this book is not about Library

2.0, it embraces many of the same principles. While some library leaders greet Library 2.0 as a radical new view of libraries, others see it as an opportunity to resurrect and refurbish ideas that have been around for quite a long time. Whichever point of view is correct, Library 2.0 is such an important development in our field that no book about customer service in libraries would be complete without a discussion of some of its basic precepts. Yet some academic librarians have embraced them, only to find that their libraries were not transformed in the ways they had hoped. Others have found that adopting the basic principles of Library 2.0 has refocused their efforts and opened up new vistas of library service. As we consider different aspects of the customer-driven library, it may become clear why libraries have had such very different outcomes.

Comparing Libraries

Before moving on to the first chapter, perhaps I should say a few words about how this book came to be written. After a twenty-five-year career in academic libraries, I retired to the "Wild" West and supposedly to a life of ease. Instead, I quickly discovered a small public library in need of a director and then a library system nestled in the foothills of the Wind River Mountains. The sea change from academic to public libraries awakened my curiosity. As I delved into public library matters, I quickly realized that both types of libraries are being challenged and even threatened. Although they differ in many ways, both must look to their customers for answers. At the same time, I was annoyed but nevertheless fascinated by the way the large bookstore chains were taking customers away from both types of libraries. Why were customers so willing to pay for the same materials they could freely enjoy at their libraries? Out of my cogitations came the book *Creating the Customer-Driven Library: Building on the Bookstore Model.* Although that book devoted considerable attention to academic libraries, it never fully considered the ways in which academic libraries are different from public libraries.

What was needed, it seemed to me, was a book that took into consideration the unique constraints within which academic librarians must work. Although the future holds challenges for public libraries, they possess considerable freedom to reinvent themselves, to morph into institutions that might not even be recognized by library patrons of the past. Academic libraries, on the other hand, function as integral parts of larger institutions. They are, to some extent, defined and controlled by others. Technology has brought rapid change to all types of libraries, but the availability of journal articles and other resources online has had a much greater impact on academic library usage than is the case with some other types of libraries.

This means that academic libraries are challenged and even threatened in ways that are different from those of public, school, and special libraries. Some naysayers even question whether the academic library as traditionally defined will survive. Declining circulation and attendance figures sound more alarm bells. Will it be possible to plot a new course that will increase the library's relevance and centrality to the academic experience? The answer, of course, lies with academic librarians themselves and with the wealth of knowledge and experience they possess. As a profession, I think that we often underestimate ourselves. When we query the general public or compare librarians with other professionals, we discover what a treasure trove of intelligence, creativity, and people skills are available to our libraries. With such paragons at the helm guided by clear, unambiguous input from their customers, academic libraries can not only survive but thrive in the twenty-first century.

1

REINVENTING THE ACADEMIC LIBRARY

Is the academic library soon to become just a virtual destination, a place in cyberspace where students access the resources that were once found only in brick-and-mortar libraries? Although librarians have argued loudly that there's far more to a library than a collection of documents, whether paper or digital, some disturbing trends are becoming apparent.

SAD TIDINGS

In 2001 Scott Carlson wrote the landmark article "The Deserted Library," which appeared in the *Chronicle of Higher Education*.[1] He cited dramatic decreases in library usage like the University of Idaho's 20 percent drop in gate count and circulation over a three-year period. At Augusta State University, gate counts dropped from 402,361 visitors to 271,977 over an eight-year period. Carlson cited other plummeting usage figures from the University of South Carolina, Texas Christian University, the University of California, the State University of New York, and the University of Maryland. Since the publication of that article, many statistical indicators of library use have continued to decline. Charles Martell followed up on Carlson's findings in his 2005 article "The Ubiquitous User: A Reexamination of Carlson's Deserted Library." He writes: "The evidence suggests that declines in the number of circulation, reserve, in-house, and reference transactions are deeper and more widespread than generally recognized. Are the declines likely to continue? Probably yes."[2] More recent articles support his prediction.

A WORST-CASE SCENARIO

It's difficult to talk about academic libraries in general because they are so very different from one another. They range from a small community college library the size of a few classrooms to a mammoth edifice like Berkeley or Harvard. To make it a little easier to discuss the problems facing academic libraries, I will wave my magic wand and create one that, like the story of

1

"The Three Bears," is neither too large nor too small. Unlike the children's story, however, it is not "just right." In the course of collecting research for this book, I have visited a great many libraries, so I'll simply borrow a few details from several of them and identify my creation as a medium-sized university library.

If I'm going to create a library, however, I had better create some students as well. Sharon will be a sophomore who's been assigned a project that requires several sources that are only available in the library. Until now, Sharon has managed to avoid the library. Although it is true that she has occasionally needed an online reserve or searched a periodical database, none of her courses have required in-library use. Sharon remembers as a freshman seeing flyers about library workshops, but she decided that she could probably get along without them. It turned out that she was quite right. Now, however, Sharon must bite the bullet and investigate the library.

Vast Unfriendly Spaces

Beyond the imposing entrance, Sharon discovers a huge echoing lobby, neutral in color and neutral in atmosphere. Stone or ceramic tiles cause footsteps to ring hollowly through the space. Graffiti-resistant walls, or perhaps cinder block, further amplify the cold, uninviting atmosphere. Although most of the space is open and empty, it may contain student lockers, rarely used (and possibly out-of-order) telephones, and plaques listing contributors to the library building fund. Possibly the literature rack once held library maps, but it is now filled with pizza ads. Sharon is carrying a large backpack and needs to set it down and get her bearings. Ideally, she needs a comfortable chair in which to rest for a few moments, open her bag, and read over her assignment. In other words, she is in a strange place and needs to focus her thoughts and make her plans before she gets to work. However, no seating area is visible. Sharon will need to rely on her memory of the assignment for the time being and may waste her time looking for the wrong materials.

The Large and Impersonal Library

To one side of the lobby area, there is an opening in the wall filled by a large circulation counter. Because several patrons are checking out materials, Sharon waits in line to ask where she might find the psychology books. However, since the student worker she asks is another undergraduate who knows little more about the library than she, Sharon is really wasting her time. Whatever question she asks, she will probably be waved vaguely toward a set of double doors. Actually, the student worker has rarely gone beyond those doors herself. Her training has focused almost entirely on assisting customers leaving the library. The focus of that training has been the online circulation module, since computer errors can cause both customers and staff endless frustration. If this work-study student were more experienced, Sharon might be encouraged to find the reference librarian or something called an OPAC. In either case, however, Sharon would be left on her own in a very large, very confusing building. Beyond the double doors indicated by the student worker is a vast space filled with stack ranges, tables, and study carrels. Signs are mainly of the "Do Not" variety, cautioning patrons to turn off their cell phones, observe library rules, and speak softly. There are other signs too, but they're difficult to see and written in a language that Sharon doesn't understand; they contain words like *periodicals, microforms,* and *circulation.* Since most of these signs lack directional arrows, they might not be very helpful to Sharon even if she understood the foreign language.

The Importance of Creature Comforts

Actually, what Sharon is really looking for now is a restroom. She's come directly from class, and creature comforts are her greatest need. Some libraries are fortunate enough to have restrooms easily visible from the entrance lobby. This one doesn't. The restroom locations were chosen by architects who found themselves dealing with small spaces created by needed structural elements and barriers. No matter where these small spaces happened to be located, they tended to be designated as restrooms. The nearest restroom in this library is down a poorly marked hallway. Many people, especially young women, are reluctant to ask for restroom directions and so may traverse much of the building before reaching their destination. Even if they are willing to ask for help, a public service desk may be as difficult to locate as a restroom.

Bear in mind that Sharon is tired. She has been carrying a heavy backpack across campus and she was unable to find a comfortable chair in the lobby. Now she's even more tired and her mood is going steadily downhill. I think we tend to forget how large our libraries really are. Because we are familiar with the library floor plan and the arrangement of materials, we tend to go directly to whatever it is we're looking for. Library users lack our experience and spend a great deal of their time walking around. Because university campuses are also very large and parking spaces are scarcer than hens' teeth, often located on the periphery of the campus, a visit to the library can be utterly exhausting.

In addition to size, what makes it especially difficult to find one's way around an academic library are the endless expanses of tall stack ranges. Typically seven or even eight feet tall, they function as room dividers, slicing the library into hundreds of small rooms, none of which is visible to the others. This means that libraries need much more carefully positioned and targeted signage than other large buildings. A sign that can be seen from one angle may be totally invisible to library users approaching from a different direction. Even signs suspended from the ceiling may be blocked by stack ranges.

However, we are forgetting about Sharon, who has finally found a restroom. Unfortunately, she is now looking on her library visit as an unpleasant experience like navigating an obstacle course, not as an inviting way to spend her time. Though her enthusiasm has waned, her assignment will be due in a few days, so she must begin locating materials. Her assignment sheet, which she has finally been able to abstract from her bag, tells her she must first view a DVD that has been placed on reserve. She has no idea what *reserve* means, but she recalls seeing a sign when she was looking for a restroom. After standing in the wrong line for several minutes, and then standing in the right line for a few more, she is told that yes, the DVD is available. However, she must check it out, view it in the audiovisual area, and return it within two hours.

Sharon then spends more time and energy walking, this time searching for the audiovisual area. Here she discovers a grand total of four DVD/TV stations. Three are in use and one has an "Out of Order" sign taped to the television monitor. She returns to the reserve desk, explains that no equipment is available, and asks to take the DVD home. Yes, overnight checkout is permitted for this item, but it may not be checked out until 6:00 p.m. It is now 2:00 p.m., and Sharon has no intention of remaining in the library a moment longer than necessary. Besides, she will be working this evening at her part-time job. Perhaps she can stop by after class tomorrow, but if the program is still unavailable, she will just have to do without it.

Next, Sharon's assignment requires that she locate an article in a reference work. This means that she will need to use the library's OPAC (online public access catalog). Because she has good computer skills, the OPAC is by far the easiest and most pleasant part of Sharon's library experience. Although library automation vendors tend to rely on older technology and their search engines may be somewhat more confusing than Google, it is not difficult to obtain the needed call number. Unfortunately, Sharon has not yet learned that reference books are not shelved with circulating books; those designations are meaningless to her. This library's OPAC program is like some others in that locations and call numbers reside in separate files; the two chunks of information come together on the display screen, but it is easy to miss the location indicator altogether.

The Invisible Library Staff

Almost any library staff member could interpret the OPAC record for Sharon, but none is in sight. It is relatively inexpensive to install OPAC stations throughout the library, but library staff are not similarly available. Most library staff members are working behind office walls and are not visible to the public. Had Sharon discovered a helpful staff member immediately upon entering the library, she could have saved herself a great deal of time, but studies indicate that most library users have little interaction with the library staff. If we accept the fact that the library building is confusing and customers often fail to find what they are seeking, if we are aware that our surveys indicate that few library users approach the reference or information desk, then why don't alarm bells ring? Why aren't we aware that we have a serious problem?

Outdated Signage

However, we have lost sight of Sharon again. She has discovered a large glass cabinet containing a professionally produced building directory. However, it turns out that several collections have been relocated since the directory was installed. The directory is out-of-date because it is difficult to make changes to it. In other words, it was designed as if the library were frozen in time, not a vital, changing organism. Sharon is fortunate this time, however, because the location shown is still accurate. She discovers that her books should be on something called a "mezzanine," but there is no such button on the elevator panel. On the wall beside the bank of three elevators, a tattered paper sign once announced the levels at which each elevator stopped. However, the sign has long since disappeared.

Sharon almost gives up after finding that her reference work is not shelved with the circulating books, but if she admits defeat, she will be unable to complete two important parts of her assignment. "Biting the bullet," she returns to the main floor and at last locates a reference librarian. As we experienced library pros would naturally expect, the reference collection is located near the reference desk, and so Sharon quickly finds what she is looking for. Again, as we old-timers know, Sharon is unable to check out a reference work, and so she must make a photocopy of the needed article.

Ignoring Customer Convenience

At this point, I can't resist telling you the story of a friend who recently returned to her alma mater after many years' absence. It so happens that hers is one of the most prestigious universities in the United States—not a midsize university like Sharon's, but a real lollapalooza. The grants, endowments, and other funding that pour into this university library would make most of us green with envy. A Ph.D. and distinguished alumna, my friend was able to use both the library's collections and its public computers.

On discovering an especially interesting online article, she sought out a printer, only to make a distressing discovery. A printout would require a printing card, a staff member explained. Printing cards were available from a machine in another department. Finally discovering the right area after a series of misadventures, my friend still had trouble locating the poorly marked card machine. You probably know where this story is going; the machine was out of order. Another machine on the fourth floor accepted only the most pristine currency, not the wadded bills she had been carrying around in her fanny pack. All campus public printers, however, accepted the same type of card. By simply walking a block to an administration building, ascending the stairs, purchasing the required print card, and retracing the path back to the library, my friend could have her article. Instead, she jotted down the citation, intending to request it from her local public library. Unfortunately, the slip of paper was lost on the journey home, and the article has since been forgotten.

Because Sharon is a student, she already has a One Card or "super card" that can be used for a variety of university services. These cards constitute a huge improvement over the systems in use in the past. Students who want to make photocopies are no longer required to produce the correct change or wait in line to pay for their copies at a service desk. However, the copy cards do not relieve the library staff of all responsibility. From the moment when they first arrived at our libraries, we have considered tending to printers and copy machines our least favorite duties. However, they are an inescapable part of the contemporary library experience, and many users come to view the library through the lens of an unpleasant encounter with them. The friend described above might have awed me with the wonders of the library's magnificent collection, but it was the printing card experience that she remembered most clearly.

It is only on her second try that Sharon finds a photocopy machine loaded with both paper and toner. Nevertheless, she is beginning to feel a little better about the library. The reference librarian was very friendly and gave her a lot of useful tips. Sharon wishes she had discovered him when she first arrived, but then she had never heard the title *reference librarian* before. Librarians, yes; she had met librarians in her public and high school libraries. In fact, she probably thought of everyone who worked in a library as a librarian. What makes a reference librarian different, she wonders?

The Evolution of Reference

Sharon was fortunate to encounter the genuine article, an honest-to-goodness professional librarian who spends a considerable part of his work-week at the reference desk. In preparing to write this book, I visited a large number of academic libraries (in fact, I recently discovered that I had five of those printer cards in my wallet, each with a few dollars' credit that I shall probably never be able to use). All the libraries I visited had a reference desk or some facsimile (although a few were unstaffed and it looked as if this might be a permanent condition). Libraries have become more complex and confusing than they were when we ourselves were students. At first glance, however, many things are simpler. The old card catalog was positively demonic with its unintuitive filing rules and unlikely subject headings. It almost took a master's degree to find a book, and only librarians and experienced researchers could discover resources that did not appear to be listed in the catalog.

Over the years, libraries were forced to develop their procedures in isolation, as if they were located somewhere in outer space. As a profession, we tend to be more detail-oriented than most others, and this isolation encouraged the development of elaborate and sometimes obtuse procedures. Because no one did things quite the way libraries did, librarians were essential as interpreters or translators. When libraries entered cyberspace, a wonderful thing happened. Computers handled details even better than librarians, but they insisted on uniformity. Not only were they ideally suited to libraries, but they imposed order and uniform procedures that everyone, whether a library or corporation or government agency, was forced to accept. Suddenly, libraries spoke the same language as their users, and users could identify resources almost as efficiently as librarians. It was then that the profession began talking about the death of reference.

Before we conclude, however, that computers have made reference skills obsolete, consider Sharon and her fellow students. They must deal with

traditional books and e-books, printed journals, microforms, article databases, virtual libraries, videos, DVDs, CDs, and a wide variety of other for-
mats. No wonder they want to query Google and accept whatever Google
delivers. In the good old days, we had much less information available to us,
but it was mostly reliable information. We were never subjected to the sheer
garbage and half-truths that confront today's students.

Whether we call it reference or information services or something else
entirely, libraries are not providing enough of it. We're spinning our wheels
worrying about whether questions are worthy of our librarians' attention
when students are scarcely aware of our existence. We're failing to convince
our users that they need us. Before she leaves the library, Sharon will have
walked more than a mile and will have encountered perhaps a dozen different library collections. However, she will leave the library with the impression that it is almost empty of staff members.

Things have been going better for Sharon, and she is now clutching a
brochure that includes a library floor plan and other useful information. Remember, however, that she is even more tired than when she arrived. The
many "dead ends" she has mistakenly pursued have left her with very little
energy. Despite an hour of searching, she has only obtained one of the resources listed on her assignment sheet. After her brief chat with the reference librarian, however, she is confident that she can locate the next items on
her list. Would that this were so! Although most of the articles she needs are
available online, her assignment includes a regional journal that is available
only in print. Her floor plan indicates that the entire third floor is devoted
to periodicals. Thanks to the reference librarian, Sharon even understands
that a "periodical" is usually a magazine or journal and that the issue she is
seeking has been bound with other issues into a hardback volume. Both of
these vital bits of information have stymied thousands of students, but
unfortunately Sharon isn't out of the woods yet.

Wasted Space

Actually, this analogy of being lost in the woods is a pretty accurate one.
When Sharon reaches the third floor, she does indeed feel as if she's in a vast
and forbidding forest. However, it's not trees but endless stack ranges that
cause her anxiety. In this library all journals, regardless of subject matter, are
shelved in A-to-Z order. The stack ranges go on and on, seemingly for miles.
Sharon thinks it will be easy to find her title, in this case a journal that her
assignment sheet lists as *CJER*. Just finding the letter *C* is tiresome because
this university library continues to store all its back runs—both the journals
available online and the most esoteric titles—in this prime space.

Most of these volumes have been replaced, first by microfiche and then by online article databases. No more than 10 percent of the printed journal collection is actually used or needed. Nevertheless, the library is holding on to many of its bound volumes "just in case." After all, the journals cost a fortune and they've scarcely been used. Some university libraries even continue to bind recent issues, even though there is little possibility that online databases will ever cease to exist. What Sharon has encountered is a huge plot of "prime real estate" that has become little more than a wasteland. However, it is not the wasted space or unjustified expense that is worrying Sharon. It is the total absence of library users or library staff members. We have all become more concerned about safety issues in public places, and we feel uncomfortable in an empty, shadowy space where any number of miscreants could hide.

Once Sharon gets the hang of the alphabetical arrangement, it is easy enough to find the letter C. However, CJER is not there. Sharon walks back and forth between stack ranges until she is totally bewildered. No staff member seems to be assigned to the floor, although there is an unstaffed service desk near the elevator. If Sharon were able to check the library's holdings at an OPAC workstation, she might find CJER listed as a cover title even though it is not the official title of the journal. However, the one OPAC she locates has lost its link to the library network, so she has no way of discovering that CJER is known to libraries as the California Journal of Educational Research.

Had Sharon encountered even a well-trained student worker at that service desk, she would probably have had her journal in a matter of minutes. Even if Sharon's question were a more difficult one, the student could call down to the reference desk. Instead, Sharon has found herself abandoned in a rather frightening place. Although there are scores of study carrels, none appear to be occupied. A homeless man seems to be asleep in one of the lounge chairs, but the only student Sharon encountered left the area soon after she arrived. This is it, Sharon decides. She has done all that she can reasonably be expected to do. Maybe another student has made a copy of the article. Maybe she can just tell her instructor that it wasn't in the library. However she deals with her problem, in the future she will avoid the library.

CUSTOMER SERVICE AND THE FUTURE OF THE ACADEMIC LIBRARY

What's wrong with simply accepting the academic library as it is? Is it really that bad? After all, lots of customers do eventually find what they need there. Unfortunately, the library environment is changing rapidly, and so there's no possibility of just treading water. The library is being swept along with the current of change, either willingly or unwillingly. In fact, change is impacting academic libraries even more than society as a whole. According to surveys by the Association of College and Research Libraries, many of the traditional measures of library activity indicate a decline in library use. Those academic libraries that are prospering have been evolving deliberately and rapidly to keep pace with both their universities and with society at large.

Examining the Customer Experience

In the past few years, an intriguing term, *Library 2.0,* has come up again and again at academic library conferences. Its inspirations, Web 2.0 and to some extent Business 2.0, had been gaining momentum in the information technology (IT) community, and it quickly became clear that the same principles could be applied to library services. At the center of all three of these developments is the belief that information professionals must partner with their users to be successful in the future. In other words, the most effective way to improve library or other services is to let customers participate in their development. We must stop making assumptions about what customers need and let them design their own services. Because its basic tenets originated in the IT community, Library 2.0 is especially concerned with improving the customer's online experience. However, it is also possible to apply Library 2.0 to the customer's experience in a real-world, brick-and-mortar academic library.

The cyber environment makes it somewhat easier to work collaboratively with customers because there are so many opportunities for online communication. Blogs, wikis, instant messaging, "social software," and other forms of digital communication are readily available. Libraries have begun to embrace some of them, but as we will find later in this book, they often surround their efforts with so many limitations and restrictions that they might just as well not bother at all. When it comes to face-to-face communication within the library building, our efforts may be even more limited. How is it possible to harness Sharon's experience in order to improve the quality of library services? Library 2.0 enthusiasts find this question a difficult one, and easy answers are hard to come by.

Customers as Individuals

Although we shouldn't need Library 2.0 to do this, the new paradigm can certainly help us refocus our attention on our customers. To better serve Sharon's needs, the first thing we must do is look on Sharon the individual as being important, really important. Traditionally, we have viewed students like Sharon as merely part of the vast sea of student library users. Because we viewed them only in the aggregate, we looked for what you might call mega-patterns. For example, we have long been able to predict ebbs and flows in library use based on the academic semester. Although we seldom use this information very effectively, we have at least been collecting it for many years. Sharon thus becomes a tick mark on the reference librarian's statistics form, a blip on the people counter at the front door.

Sometimes, however, we manage to get a little closer to understanding Sharon's needs. We still concern ourselves with the aggregate, rather than with Sharon herself, but we've developed some postulates about what resources psychology students use, and we certainly have a lot of firmly held beliefs about beginning students. Many of these beliefs, however, tend to be somewhat negative. "Business students never bring books back on time." "Physical education students are brain-dead and never read signs." If we work with faculty members, we may learn more from them. For example, when faculty let us know about an upcoming assignment ahead of time, we can be better prepared. In fact, such advance preparation might have helped Sharon in her hour of need. Faculty know how their students behave in the classroom; they know their strengths, limitations, and work habits when seen in that environment. However, they do not really know how students use the library.

If we made an effort to know Sharon better, we would discover dozens of things about her that may not be typical of other undergraduate students. For example, Sharon's time constraints are important. She is working her way through college and is finding time management difficult. Because she is only beginning to understand how to organize her time, she is always hurrying, always feeling harried. Sharon has, to a large extent, overcome the dyslexia that once made reading so difficult and embarrassing, but she can easily transpose words and numbers when she is tired. Although she is quite intelligent, she may misunderstand the meaning of signs and may feel more comfortable getting directions from a staff member. However, she is somewhat shy and uncomfortable with authority figures. Like most freshman and sophomore students, Sharon knows absolutely nothing about the world of scholarly publishing and finds it difficult to even conceive of the thousands of scholarly journals that libraries collect. She is neither familiar with their terminology, nor with their volume numbers, nor with their tendency to use acronyms as titles in some situations and complete titles in others. All of this is in-crowd knowledge that Sharon lacks, but only Sharon knows how the library can fit into her world.

Customers as Full Partners

In future chapters, we will spend quite a lot of time considering ways in which we can bring Sharon and other students into our planning and make them active participants in the library's future. Difficult though it may be, we can increase both virtual and face-to-face communication between individual student customers and members of the library staff, making effective use of the treasure trove of information we glean. However, for now, I want to emphasize how essential this communication is to the survival and successful evolution of the library as both a place and an effective information provider. As Sharon traversed her university library, she found it almost devoid of library staff members. However, if we were able to obtain a copy of the library's staff directory, we would probably find well over one hundred names listed there. This means that most library staff have little contact with customers, no matter what is written in their job descriptions. In a library like Sharon's, customer service may be little more than a few lines of boiler-plate language divorced from real-world duties and responsibilities.

The Library Staff and Library Renewal

There is no way that the handful of people who actually work with customers can, all by themselves, embark on the difficult task of transforming the academic library. Whether librarians, administrators, paraprofessionals, or computer technicians, many more staff members will be needed. Of course, when this subject comes up during library meetings, many will express their ideas. However, only those who possess the skill, determination, and courage to partner with students and faculty can effectively redesign the library. The job obviously requires the talents of the best and the brightest on the library staff. Judging from the way we hire, train, and supervise our most visible public service staff, the members of the circulation department, we have a long, long way to go. Creating a customer-driven library will require a complete reassessment of library priorities, and achieving these priorities will, in turn, require a complete reassessment of staff resources.

Radical Trust

So how does Library 2.0 recommend that we partner with Sharon to improve the quality of library services? In real life, we can't follow her on her library odyssey, even though such an experience would probably result in dozens of ideas for improving library services. Since that is not possible, how can we find out what has gone wrong with Sharon's experience? Sharon is, of course, only one individual. How can we obtain the same information from all those other students who may have had totally different experiences? The logical answer is that Sharon and her peers will have to tell us what they need and how they have experienced the library. Otherwise, we're still guessing; we're still depending on those unsubstantiated beliefs about our customers.

Yet many of us have frequently been guilty of making disparaging comments about Sharon and her peers, criticizing their work habits, their language, their music, their interests, and, of course, their ignorance of the library. One of the most important concepts of Library 2.0 is *radical trust*. This term refers to the willingness of library decision makers to trust their customers to help them redefine and redesign the library. Even though Sharon is very young, inexperienced, and uninformed about many subjects, we must trust her to know what she needs. As information professionals, we possess sophisticated research skills, but Sharon knows herself and her own world. If we can bring our two worlds together, we may come up with some very revolutionary ideas about library service. Radical trust means acting on those revolutionary ideas even if they contradict what we think we know about libraries.

Constraints on the Library

Weighed down by the daily struggle to balance the budget, do the work of two or more staff members, and satisfy conflicting demands, academic librarians may think they have little time for revitalizing the library. Simply coping with the library as it is seems far too demanding to waste time envisioning it as it can and should be. However, if the future is to be a sunny one, it is necessary to step back, temporarily separate ourselves from the daily drama, and envision our vital, dynamic future library.

Of course, academic libraries are limited in their power to reinvent themselves by the demands of the academic environment. Revolutionary ideas must pass the test of real-world scrutiny. First and foremost, libraries must work in harmony with the academic program, providing materials that supplement the classroom experience and support faculty and student research. Libraries also function as administrative departments, constrained by rules, procedures, and competition for scarce resources. They may have very limited control over their own budgets and feel compelled to meet the expectations of decision makers who know nothing about libraries. This does not mean, however, that libraries are unable to determine how they will fulfill their missions. The library's customers can serve as a sort of compass, pointing libraries toward the future. By focusing on the needs of their customers, libraries can create an environment that is physically inviting, intellectually stimulating, and a focal point to which all members of the academic community are drawn.

NOTES

1. Scott Carlson, "The Deserted Library: As Students Work Online, Reading Rooms Empty Out—Leading Some Campuses to Add Starbucks," *Chronicle of Higher Education,* November 16, 2001, A35; available at http://chronicle.com/free/v48/i12/12a03501.htm.
2. Charles R. Martell, "The Ubiquitous User: A Reexamination of Carlson's Deserted Library," *portal: Libraries and the Academy* 5, no. 4 (October 2005): 441.

RESOURCES

Carlson, Scott. "The Deserted Library: As Students Work Online, Reading Rooms Empty Out—Leading Some Campuses to Add Starbucks." *Chronicle of Higher Education,* November 16, 2001, 35. Available at http://chronicle.com/free/v48/i12/12a03501.htm.

Council on Library and Information Resources. *Library as Place: Rethinking Roles, Rethinking Space.* CLIR Publication no. 129. Washington, DC: Council on Library and Information Resources, 2005. Available at www.clir.org/pubs/reports/pub129/pub129.pdf.

De Rosa, Cathy. *College Students' Perceptions of Libraries and Information Resources: A Report to the OCLC Membership; A Companion Piece to Perceptions of Libraries and Information Resources.* Dublin, OH: OCLC Online Computer Library Center, 2006. Available at www.oclc.org/reports/perceptionscollege.htm.

Dillon, Dennis. "College Libraries: The Long Goodbye." *Chronicle of Higher Education,* November 10, 2004, 3.

Frank, Donald G., and Elizabeth Howell. "New Relationships in Academe: Opportunities for Vitality and Relevance." *College and Research Libraries News* 64, no. 1 (January 3, 2003). Available at www.ala.org/ala/acrl/acrlpubs/crlnews/backissues2003/january03/newrelationships.cfm.

Lowry, Charles B. "When's This Paradigm Shift Ending?" *portal: Libraries and the Academy* 2, no. 1 (January 2002): 79–97.

Mangan, Katherine S. "Packing Up the Books: U. of Texas Becomes the Latest Institution to Clear Out a Main Library to Make Room for Computers." *Chronicle of Higher Education,* July 1, 2005, A27.

Neal, James G. "The Entrepreneurial Imperative: Advancing from Incremental to Radical Change in the Academic Library." *portal: Libraries and the Academy* 1, no. 1 (January 2001): 1–13.

2

MAKING IT HAPPEN

Leadership and the Professional Staff

Many long years ago when I began my academic library career, there seemed to be an extraordinary number of academic librarians. They could be found in practically every area of the library, and library customers came into frequent contact with them. During the past thirty years, the number of degreed librarians has declined in academic libraries, and paraprofessionals often manage library departments like circulation and document delivery. This sometimes works well, giving library decision makers more flexibility in hiring and assigning staff. Sometimes, however, it may mean that the few remaining librarians have little involvement in molding the library to meet the needs of its customers.

LIBRARIANS AS LEADERS

Although library directors are usually responsible for their buildings in a general sense, library assistants and paraprofessional managers make many of the decisions that determine the kind of environment students and faculty experience. One has to wonder if these libraries are fully utilizing what are perhaps their most valuable assets. Typical academic librarians are highly educated, often holding both an M.L.S. and a second master's degree. They tend to be both intelligent and intellectually curious, able to find their way in the vast reaches of the information universe. In short, they are often unusually gifted people who possess a wealth of knowledge, especially knowledge about libraries. If the academic library is to change, librarians must be at the helm, guiding it through the dangerous shoals that lie ahead.

The Public View of Librarians

Not only are fewer librarians employed in academic libraries, but less of their time is spent working with the public. Library journals have proclaimed the death of reference, and library administrators can't be blamed for wondering why it requires an M.L.S. to help students click the correct links in an online database. The result is that students rarely see or speak with a librarian in many academic libraries. Although most libraries continue to maintain a reference desk, it may be staffed by librarians who are each assigned only a few hours of desk duty a week, far less time than is needed to develop any real reference expertise. Experienced paraprofessionals and library science students may be scheduled on the desk when librarians are unavailable or have other priorities. When the reference desk is replaced by the information desk, paraprofessionals are even more likely to be the ones assisting library customers.

The Quest for Faculty Status

If librarians no longer have time for public service duty, what is it that occupies their time and assumes a higher priority? To answer this question, we must first consider the status of librarians and their quest for respect and acceptance in the academic community. Much of the history of academic librarianship charts the uphill battle for acceptance as both professionals and academics, entitled to salaries commensurate with those of teaching faculty. Librarians have long fought for full faculty status or some similar designation that takes into consideration their academic qualifications. That battle, however, has not been going well. As Todd Gilman puts it in an article in the *Chronicle of Higher Education,* "the number of institutions offering faculty status to librarians may have diminished since 1990; the vogue for offering librarians faculty status was already on the decline back then."[1]

The resulting sense of loss and the damage inflicted on academic librarians' sense of identity has tended to further focus our profession on academic status and achievements. Job descriptions inevitably reflect this professional insecurity. The duties and responsibilities included in them are often designed to support librarians in their struggle. For example, library instruction holds a high priority not only because information literacy is an important library value, but also because it mirrors the work of the teaching faculty. Intellectually challenging tasks like building digital libraries, presenting papers at conferences, preparing pathfinders and subject guides, and supporting geographical information systems can also help establish one's claim to being academically respectable.

The Needs of the Library versus the Needs of Librarians

Because teaching faculty are required to publish scholarly articles in peer-reviewed journals, academic librarians are usually required or encouraged to publish as well. The problem is, however, that librarians are already putting in a forty-hour workweek, while time for writing and research is, at least to some extent, understood to be part of the teaching faculty's normal schedule. Since it is unfair for librarians to be expected to take so much of their own personal time to meet faculty standards for promotion and tenure, they are often given time to work on publications during their workday. Since one cannot write a journal article without having something to write about, some program must be designed, implemented, and evaluated. The kinds of library activities that lend themselves to research projects are necessarily limited. Thus, it is not unusual for librarians to spend considerable time working on projects that may ultimately be of little value to their libraries.

Nearly all academic libraries have a mission statement that focuses on service to the academic community. These statements are filled with phrases like "serve the needs of," "inform and empower students," and "provide user-focused services." Academic librarians take their mission very seriously, but they must also consider competing demands. Managing a library department like document delivery, for example, may give them the opportunity to redirect library services to better meet customer needs. But then they ask: Is managing a department really an academic function? Would the teaching faculty view a manager as a colleague?

Take another example, the circulation department. Depending on the size and priorities of the library, it is common to find that the circulation manager is not a librarian. The justification for this practice may be an assumption that the kind of expertise the degreed librarian possesses is not needed. Yet most of the interaction that students and faculty have with the library is with the circulation staff. Even teaching faculty members may assume that the staff member behind the circulation desk, especially the circulation supervisor, is a librarian and base their opinion of the library on that staff member. Teaching faculty may ultimately view librarians with less respect, while the library itself suffers from their absence in key roles. Although many library paraprofessionals develop considerable expertise over the years, it is usually confined to one aspect of the library's operation and may be at odds with other library goals and priorities. In other words, the supervisors who largely determine the way in which the library interacts with the academic community may possess little real understanding of the library or its mission.

A Library That Bucked the Trend

A year or two ago, I visited a rather large academic library that occupies a building consisting of several floors. In many similar libraries, I might expect to find public service librarians only on the main level. When I ascended to the third and fourth floors, however, in addition to the usual service desks, I discovered small information stations—two or more on each level. What a large staff! I thought. As it turned out, the staff was no larger than those in other comparable libraries, but many librarians and paraprofessionals spent the better part of their workday at public desks. Each information station was designed to allow them to perform their normal duties and still be available to students and faculty. Each workstation consisted of one or two typical office desks (not tall counters), a telephone, computer equipment that could be locked down for security, and low file cabinets with secure locks so staff could store both personal possessions and paperwork when they were away from their desks. Each of these office desks was assigned to one staff member, and each was used as a librarian or paraprofessional's personal work space. If the information station was staffed by more than one person, there was a desk for each. Above each station, a large sign hung from the ceiling. Customers could usually see an "Information" sign from almost anywhere on the floor.

As you'll discover in later chapters, this library made a profound impact on me. Like other twenty-first-century academic libraries I visited, it suffered from a number of maladies, but this single innovation made an extraordinary difference in customers' perceptions of the library. I learned that the program began with a decision made by public service librarians after the university newspaper printed an especially negative article about the library. If librarians and experienced paraprofessionals were more visible, they would have far more influence on customer perceptions of the library.

Initially, the challenge was to learn to perform normal duties from remote public areas. The staff kept all their equipment, supplies, and materials at their information stations, but they could make use of enclosed office areas when they needed greater privacy to write a report or make a phone call. However, these were not private offices; it was understood that they were only to be used for special situations. To minimize the sense of isolation from other staff members, everyone made frequent use of instant messaging (IM) programs. Although telephones were available at all information stations, there was something about the informality of messaging that helped staff feel connected. The staff got to know their areas very well. However, when questions were beyond their expertise, both they and their customers frequently messaged a reference librarian.

Defining a Librarian

Perhaps it would be a good idea at this point to say a few words about library education and professional staffing. Twenty years ago, there was almost no question about just what a librarian was. Although the public might assume that anyone encountered behind a service desk was a librarian, we ourselves had a reasonably clear definition of the term. In the United States, at any rate, a librarian possessed a master's degree in library science from an academic program accredited by the American Library Association. Curricula varied little from one program to another. Although some were more high-tech than others, all prepared their students to assume professional positions in a school, public, special, or academic library.

Of course, to some extent, this definition is still applicable. What has changed, however, is that today's "information professionals" may now find themselves in jobs that bear almost no resemblance to one another and may seem totally unrelated to any courses they took in library school. In academic libraries, the gap between professionals who work in an almost totally digital world and those who concern themselves with bewildered freshmen has widened to the point that they appear to be engaged in totally different professions. This dichotomy, of course, poses serious problems for library education, because most programs are poorly funded and find it difficult to meet the needs of such a diverse profession. Another problem created by this situation may be more damaging, however. Almost inevitably, questions arise about who the real information professionals are. Those involved in database development or digital library projects must possess sophisticated and clearly identifiable skills to do their work effectively. Their involvement with technology adds a cachet that tends to further elevate their status.

On the other hand, the professionals who work in a world of brick and mortar possess less readily defined skills. For example, they need reference skills, but not in the same sense as librarians of yore. Those paragons guided their patrons through vast and largely uncharted terrain consisting of innumerable catalogs, directories, indices, bibliographies, concordances, Festschrifts, and other cryptic and highly individualistic references that could only be interpreted by the library cognoscenti. Today's academic librarians need to understand the organization of knowledge, but little original cataloging is performed in most academic libraries. Instead, the knowledge needed has more to do with the university curriculum and reading the minds of inarticulate students who have no idea how the topic of their research fits into this information universe. To make matters even worse, insecurity about faculty status may make librarians hesitate to identify the job of providing a comfortable, pleasant environment for library customers as a professional responsibility.

Librarians Must Be Leaders

If academic libraries are to survive and prosper, we must find a way out of this kind of destructive mind-set. The vitally important work of guiding a library and enabling it to meet the needs of its customers must be viewed with respect. The term *professional* has defined librarianship for too long to abandon it, but redefinition has become essential. In the past, we tended to equate *complicated* with *professional.* Cataloging was complicated and, therefore, professional. In fact, we probably made it more complicated than necessary in order to better deserve professional status. Reference was complicated because it required knowledge of thousands of information sources, each organized in its own unique and eccentric way.

Because librarians earn higher salaries than paraprofessionals, administrators are forced to justify the expense by proving that librarians are really engaged in professional duties. Unfortunately, most definitions of professionalism take little cognizance of the library's mission or the needs of its users. One might think that the higher-paid staff members were those who were most involved in achieving the library's mission, but this may not be true. In fact, there may actually be a disconnect between high-status activities and mission-focused activities.

PROFESSIONALISM AND LEADERSHIP

Would it clarify matters to define library professionals as leaders? Can we define professionals as those individuals who possess the experience, education, and skills needed to lead the library toward its most important goals— service to the academic community and a central role in the educational process? As I write these words, I am reminded of a visit to a large university library and an interview conducted with a public service librarian whom I will call Linda. We met in Linda's cubicle in what was called the librarians' corral. Later in the afternoon, she would take a two-hour shift at the reference desk, but before I arrived, she had been preparing a political science pathfinder. (Librarians were assigned disciplines for the purpose of book selection, library instruction, and related activities. Political science was one of her assigned disciplines.) Although this was a sizable university library, a budget cut had reduced the number of degreed librarians. Paraprofessionals now managed several public service functions, and librarians tended to spend the better part of their workdays in the librarians' corral.

Now I have nothing against pathfinders, but it is possible to find a plethora of good ones online. Of course, each library has somewhat different resources, but basic databases and reference sources are common to most academic libraries. Linda's desk was cluttered with her work: professional journals, book review sources, a draft of an article she was writing (required for promotion), a contribution to the library website, notes from the meeting of a minor university committee (why is it librarians are so often chosen as committee secretaries?), and a telephone message from a faculty member who would not be able to meet with her. As we talked, I was struck by what an intelligent, articulate woman she was.

Sidelined Librarians

Here was a highly educated and seemingly very competent librarian who appeared to have little or no role in leading the library. She spent most of her day performing useful tasks that would make little difference to either the library or the university at large. At the same time, staff members with less education, little understanding of the library's mission, and lower salaries managed some public service departments. If one were to ask who was serving in a leadership role, it certainly would not be Linda. She spent much of her time in the librarians' corral, had little contact with most of the library staff, was assigned no supervisory responsibilities, and impacted library policies and procedures only through her input at staff and librarians' meetings.

Although Linda's was one of the higher salaries in the library, her talents were being largely wasted. Here was a personable, talented, and highly trained staff member whose influence on the library was negligible. She produced excellent pathfinders and did a nice job when she taught the occasional library literacy class. When she attended librarians' meetings, she offered good ideas, but topics for discussion were so limited that her ideas had little effect on the library as a whole. To be perfectly truthful, she wasn't even a very good reference librarian, because she didn't spend enough hours on the desk to become proficient. Could it be that a mistaken notion of professionalism was preventing Linda from fully participating in the achievement of the library's goals?

Leadership by Default

That same day I met with Richard, the hardworking head of circulation. Although this was once a professional position, it was reclassified a few years ago during one of the library's periodic budget crunches. The university

administrator who reclassified the position was given a definition of a professional librarian by the library director, who also provided a list of sample
duties. The list had been created to support the librarians' quest for faculty
status and was intended to make the work of librarians resemble as much as
possible that of teaching faculty members. Naturally, it didn't seem as if the
circulation head performed many of these duties.

The position was then reclassified and posted internally for university
personnel. One of the applicants was Richard, a young man who worked in
the university business office, had a little supervisory experience, and possessed an associate's degree. Union rules gave him priority over outsiders,
and there were no interested, qualified library staff applicants. Because he
received glowing evaluations, he was hired for the job. Richard was a quick
learner, got along well with other staff members, and kept the circulation department humming. Overdue notices went out on time, fines were collected
accurately, and library resources were circulated efficiently.

After meeting him, I realized that by default, Richard had become one of
the library's chief decision makers. While I sat beside his desk with notebook
in hand, he stood at the office door. We were interrupted constantly by people demanding his attention. A circulation staff member needed permission
to forgive a fine, a plumber required a command decision about a restroom
sink, a librarian needed a classroom, a part-time faculty member was in a
stew. Most of these matters were routine in nature, but I soon realized that
Richard was also making decisions about the location of library collections,
the hours when the online system could be shut down for maintenance, the
vendor to be awarded a library contract, the chairs to be purchased for the
new faculty studies, and the hours of the library café. Someone, perhaps a
custodian, staff member, faculty member, or vendor, would arrive at the
circulation desk, ask a question, and ultimately receive an answer from
Richard. Grateful that their problems had been resolved, they continued to
seek him out, either in person or by phone, each time they needed an answer.
I never sensed that Richard had a Napoleon complex; he just wanted to be
helpful, settle the issue, and get back to his own work.

The problem was that Richard knew little about the library or its goals,
and he viewed students as the source of many of his problems. Students did
not bring books back on time; students spilled coffee on the library carpet.
Of course, they were nice enough in their way, but his job was certainly a lot
easier during break periods. When idealistic notions about customer service
were discussed at meetings, Richard always gave the lip service he knew was
required. However, he really thought the librarians lived in a dream world,
unaware of what was really going on in the library.

Where Decisions Are Made

Both Richard's and Linda's positions came under the administrative umbrella of the assistant director, Ruth, who was primarily responsible for the internal operation of the library. In our brief meeting, Ruth told me that Richard was a godsend. She didn't know what she'd do if he weren't there to keep the library running smoothly. Ruth didn't know Linda nearly as well as she knew Richard. Of course, she had heard Linda speak at professional meetings, but her mind was often on something else at those meetings. They tended to be dull and people argued interminably. As we all know, that tends to be the nature of meetings. Good decisions may come out of them, but they are always made slowly and with difficulty.

Because both the library director and the assistant director believed in teamwork, they made a point of involving the librarians in at least some of the major policy decisions. Every day, however, smaller policy decisions were being made without anyone really recognizing them as such. It was only when, for example, the director received a barrage of student complaints that she realized the new library hours had been set for the convenience of the staff, causing considerable inconvenience to the library's customers. Such decisions certainly had an impact on policy, and they contributed significantly to negative attitudes about the library. Yet they were among the decisions that Assistant Director Ruth was happy to turn over to Circulation Head Richard. Of course, they might have been turned over to a committee, but when a job was given to Richard, Ruth knew it would get done and done quickly. She never quite knew what to expect from the library's many teams and committees.

What never seemed to occur to either the library director or assistant director was that a number of librarians might individually have made better decisions if they had been actively involved in day-to-day activities and held responsible for successes and failures. For just a moment, let's stand Linda and Richard side by side. Both are bright, competent, and personable. Both are respected by their peers and receive very positive performance evaluations. Linda, however, has earned a bachelor's degree in an academic subject and a master's degree in library science. She worked in her university library as a graduate assistant and has held professional positions in other academic libraries. She is a member of several professional organizations, meets regularly with her colleagues from other universities, reads professional journals, takes refresher courses to keep up-to-date with new developments, and has a deep commitment to the mission of the academic library. Richard, on the other hand, is not much interested in libraries as such. He accidentally discovered the university when he was looking for a job, was hired on by the business office, and moved over to the library when a higher-paying position became available. Richard was able to legitimately claim a little supervisory experience on his résumé, but nothing prepared him for the large staff of student workers and library staff members he now supervises. He often complains about how hard he works, not realizing that his job would be less arduous if he knew how to delegate responsibility and manage people more effectively. He feels he has no choice but to make these constant "command" decisions off the top of his head, to some extent, just to make them go away.

Assistant Director Ruth imagines that librarians would probably do a terrible job at managing circulation. That may be because she tends to see them en masse at meetings where petty disagreements and personality conflicts are common. Richard leaps into the fray and gets the job done. Although it might sound somewhat revolutionary, I think that Linda could get the job done too. Had she understood that management and supervision were "professional" responsibilities, been given gradually increasing supervisory duties, and been encouraged to consider library management part of her job description, she might even have done considerably better than Richard. Linda would know when a decision had broader implications than seemed immediately apparent. Being part of the ebb and flow of public service, she would have the insight to see the library's philosophy constantly "butting heads" with the reality of everyday crises.

The Library Culture

On the other hand, I have to sympathize with Ruth. The nature of her job, the demands of her boss, and her own good sense force her to see the library through the eyes of students and faculty. Most customer complaints eventually find their way to her desk. In fact, it is Ruth who is usually "called on the carpet" for sins and omissions at every level of library public services. Ruth sees herself as the victim of what has been called the library culture. She feels caught in the middle between a seemingly intransigent professional library staff and a director who demands trendy accomplishments that can be touted on evaluations and among colleagues. A number of authors, including John Budd, Soyeon Lee, Robert H. McDonald, and Chuck Thomas, have attempted to analyze the institutional culture that typifies many academic libraries. They use a variety of instruments, often taken from the corporate sector, to determine how the library environment compares to other workplaces.

It turns out that, in general, we are not so very different, but we may be less receptive to change. What seems to be the problem is that sometimes individual librarians establish goals and set priorities that are separate from and possibly in conflict with the library's goals and priorities. We are all aware of the stereotype of the detail-obsessed librarian. Like most stereo-types, it is a gross overgeneralization, but as a profession we do have a pro-nounced tendency to focus on the trees rather than the forest. Librarians may become so immersed in project details that project goals become lost or mired in bureaucracy. Several years ago, I participated in a focus group consisting of academic library administrators. The topic under discussion was the library culture, especially the group process in academic libraries. I discovered that the library administrators had a very negative view of pro-fessional library meetings. They appeared to believe that when librarians got together to make decisions, they made the issues far more complicated than necessary, focusing on peripheral details while major problems remained unresolved. In fact, it seemed to these administrators that librarians enjoyed weaving unlikely contingencies and extraneous possibilities into even rela-tively simple decisions.

Although I agree that there are problems with the organizational culture of many academic libraries, I wonder if library administrators do not con-tribute to their own problems. Take the case of Linda, for example. Linda has never seen herself as having any real responsibility for the management of the library. Her status as a "professional" has kept her in a kind of cocoon. She has had almost no opportunity to make decisions independently and then see how they contribute to or detract from the library's success. What she has become skilled at is attending meetings. This is not to say that she has learned to make meetings more efficient or effective. She has worked hard at developing team skills, but she has also learned to play meeting games, in other words, to view meetings almost as sporting events where points are scored and opponents clash over unimportant matters. Because she is so lit-tle involved in the everyday life of the library, she rarely sees how decisions made at meetings are actually implemented. In fact, some of those decisions may never be implemented at all, because they are often viewed as unim-portant by harassed administrators faced with real-world crises.

Taking Responsibility

Although teamwork is essential to a successful library, personal respon-sibility is even more necessary. What may have happened in some aca-demic libraries is that paraprofessional staff have assumed more personal responsibility while librarians, who do not occupy administrative positions, have relinquished personal responsibility in the name of teamwork. Most of the decisions presented to Richard require immediate action. Referring them to a team or committee might cause delays and precipitate crises. Yet many of those decisions have a significant impact on the way the library serves its customers and its success in achieving its mission. They also require precisely the kind of practical, down-to-earth experience that Richard's job provides.

While I was meeting with Linda, it struck me that she was bored with her work. Linda was an intelligent woman who had earned high grades in school and graduated near the top of her college class. In library school she had likewise distinguished herself. Now that she had achieved her goal and become a librarian, Linda was no longer challenged. Although she liked being busy and found plenty to do, not much really depended on Linda. If she took a day off, nothing terrible happened. Another librarian might have to take an additional hour or two of reference duty. Even freshman library classes are sufficiently interchangeable that someone else could take Linda's class without missing a beat. When, however, Richard stayed home from work, "all hell broke loose," as the saying goes. If a paraprofessional is so much more important to the library than a highly trained, better-paid professional, something certainly must be wrong.

RESPONDING TO THE ENVIRONMENT

Later in this book, I will write about the move that's afoot in many university libraries to embed librarians in academic departments. To some extent, this is a way of revisiting the old system of departmental libraries, but in a much more cost-effective way. Those small libraries that usually supported a single discipline were far more open to their environments than today's mega-libraries. The priorities and prejudices of the discipline circulated through them. In gathering material for this book, I have visited large libraries, small libraries, and in-between libraries. In general, I have found that the smaller the library, the more likely that it will respond to external stimuli. I certainly don't mean that small libraries are better than large libraries, and economies of size can result in more extensive customer services. What I do mean is that in small libraries, the walls of the library seem more permeable. The library is a more integral part of the academic community, and the academic community has a greater influence in determining how the library develops.

As the library grows larger, the walls become less penetrable. The external academic environment does not naturally infuse the library with its values, and the internal walls separating library functions also make the library less responsive to its community. To counteract this isolation, librarians are often encouraged to participate in university committees and task forces. As I mentioned earlier, Linda is a member of some university committees and enjoys the opportunity to meet new people and get away from the library for a few hours. This is true for most librarians, and Assistant Director Ruth (somewhat unwillingly) participates in a great many university-wide groups. Each of them has acquired a puzzle piece, a small glimpse of what is happening outside the library. The trouble is that they almost never attempt to put the puzzle pieces together. That's probably because there are always higher-priority issues that occupy their attention. Rarely do library staff members get together to discuss what's happening outside the library.

The Library's Opportunity

Yet the library is in a unique position to understand what's happening to the university as a whole. Few departments have this opportunity to piece together information from both the academic and the administrative sides of the institution. In fact, most units of the university are considerably more isolated than the library. They live in separate worlds where the walls between disciplines and between administrative functions are even less permeable than the library's. This means that librarians have a unique opportunity to assume university-wide leadership roles. Yet only very occasionally did my library visits introduce me to librarians who were real leaders and change agents in their universities. In one small college, the library director filled in when the dean of the college went on sabbatical because he was familiar with many of the issues facing the college and was regarded as objective and impartial. In a larger university, a dean of library services who had a very commanding personality frequently managed to sway the power structure. Otherwise, I encountered very few instances of librarians playing key roles in their academic institutions.

If we look in once again on Linda the public service librarian and Richard the head of circulation, I think we'll see why leadership is so rarely found among librarians. With all her experience and education, Linda was never prepared to become a leader. In library school, her single course in library management was so general that it failed to provide a basis for future responsibility. Had she interned under the library director when she was working in the library as a graduate student, she might have acquired some practical knowledge, but I found such internships to be extremely rare. Once Linda became an academic librarian, she was never evaluated on her success as a change agent who made things happen both within and outside of the library. Assistant Director Ruth was also the victim of this failure to provide leadership experiences and training. A few years ago, she graduated from a position much like Linda's to one with extensive supervisory responsibilities. There was no gradual transition to allow her to get her bearings or learn from her mistakes. Almost nothing in her education or professional experience had prepared her for her new job.

In the course of our interview, Linda described her work on several library teams. As in most academic libraries, the concept of teams assuming management responsibilities is a popular one. Unfortunately, the teams Linda described sounded a lot like old-fashioned committees. For example, team members never developed the kind of unified outlook and trust of one another that characterizes a successful team. Some team members were allowed to act out interpersonal conflicts, while others spent meetings trying to soothe hurt feelings. Just as committees have traditionally served as a way of shifting responsibility away from oneself, Linda's fellow team members sometimes went to extraordinary lengths to avoid committing themselves to what they saw as additional work.

As is often the case with committees, team members did not hold one another accountable when they failed to complete assignments. When, at long last, a decision or plan finally emerged from the group, nothing happened. The library director expressed her thanks and then it appeared that the plan was filed away. Perhaps the team had planned with little thought to budget realities; perhaps the library director had never made it clear how the resource or service would be paid for. For that matter, the plan that emerged from all those marathon meetings may have been totally unrealistic. In the business world, when a team produces an impractical plan, the individuals are held accountable. In some organizations they might even be fired or demoted. I would certainly not recommend such dire punishments, but there should be some penalty for wasting the library's time and money. Only in a Dilbert comic strip would an executive in a corporation expend considerable money to support the work of a team and then totally ignore its research and recommendations.

What was perhaps most disturbing about my interviews with administrators, librarians, and other staff at Linda's university library was that they really thought they were in the forefront of library innovation. They had read widely in both library and business literature and were well acquainted with all the current buzzwords. Because many librarians were required to publish, they made a substantial contribution to library literature, and they naturally tended to write about their own library. This was a sobering thought indeed. I could not help but think of the well-known cliché about the blind leading the blind. I'm convinced, however, that this academic library, like many others, has the potential to become a truly successful and innovative one. Its librarians are highly trained and talented people who sincerely believe in libraries. There is no question that they truly care about their customers and want to serve their needs. To achieve the essential transformation, however, every librarian in that iniquitous library corral must become a leader, and most should probably abandon the corral entirely.

NOTE

1. Todd Gilman, "Academic Librarians and Rank," *Chronicle of Higher Education,* January 4, 2008; available at http://chronicle.com/jobs/news/2008/01/2008010401c/careers.html.

RESOURCES

Carr, R. "What Users Want: An Academic 'Hybrid' Library Perspective." *Ariadne* 46 (February 2006). Available at www.ariadne.ac.uk/issue46/carr/.

Devlin, F. A., et al. "Getting beyond Institutional Cultures: When Rivals Collaborate." *Journal of Library Administration* 45, no. 1/2 (2006): 149–68.

Dewey, B. I. "Leadership and University Libraries: Building to Scale at the Interface of Cultures." *Journal of Library Administration* 42, no. 1 (2005): 41–50.

Hernon, P. *The Next Library Leadership: Attributes of Academic and Public Library Directors.* Westport, CT: Libraries Unlimited, 2003.

Hernon, P., R. R. Powell, and A. P. Young. "Academic Library Directors: What Do They Do?" *College and Research Libraries* 65, no. 6 (2004): 538–61.

Raubenheimer, J., et al. "Rethinking Leadership Roles for the Academic Library: The Attitudes of Library Staff towards a Leadership-Driven Academic Information Service Enterprise." *Mousaion* 24, no. 2 (2006): 232–48.

3

PUBLIC SERVICE STAFFING

Past, Present, and Future

Over the course of the last few decades, academic libraries have been growing larger while academic library staffs have been shrinking. Many libraries
have been successful in enlarging their buildings, sometimes adding a wing
to an existing structure or, preferably, constructing a brand-new building.
On the other hand, the need for a small army of typists, filers, and other "paper-
pushing" staff members, supervised by a somewhat smaller brigade of librarian supervisors, has largely disappeared. Computers have eliminated
the long hours of drudgery that characterized most routine library tasks.
Automated library systems have greatly simplified record-keeping; acquisitions modules communicate directly with vendors; and shared cataloging
networks have all but eliminated the need for original cataloging in many
academic libraries. During this same period, staffs have also been downsized
for budgetary reasons. The rising cost of resources, especially scholarly journals, has tended to further shrink the number of professional, paraprofessional, and clerical library positions.

THE SHRINKING LIBRARY STAFF

These trends taken together have created the sense of acres of book stacks:
vast, empty, and seemingly uncharted spaces rarely visited by the library
staff. Gradually, the library staff have become concentrated almost entirely
at two service desks, a few cubicle clusters, and a downsized "back room"
domain. Student shelvers may be the only staff members who ever visit the
far-flung reaches of the library, and in many libraries, cuts in federal funding have reduced the availability of student workers. Additionally, book circulation has declined sharply, so fewer shelvers are needed. Customers may
wander, lost and confused, through some academic libraries for half an hour
without encountering a staff member.

Considering the changes that have been taking place, it may be time
to completely reevaluate the way we staff our academic libraries. For example, computerization has driven many of the changes. Are there ways

that computers can help us improve the quality of service to our customers? Computers may have been responsible for eliminating many staff positions, but they can also make it possible to decentralize staff functions. Some libraries are discovering that computers make it possible to station more staff members in public areas because they are no longer chained to a multitude of paper files and printed resources. In fact, technology has made communication so fast and efficient that it has even become possible to station librarians outside the library for part of their workday. This chapter considers a variety of different staffing models and the impact they can have on customer service.

The Invisible Library Staff

If the library is to have a central role in the academic world, then it stands to reason that the library staff must be a visible part of that world. Yet most librarians and other library staff members are largely invisible to the academic community. In the first chapter we described the undergraduate student Sharon, whose unproductive library experience was, in part, caused by the absence of staff to assist her. To further demonstrate this point, let's peek inside another representative university library. How large is the staff of this library? If we were to search the data at the National Center for Education Statistics website, we might find a number of medium-sized university libraries, each with roughly 100–200 staff members, excluding student workers. Let's assume, therefore, that our library tour will focus on one of these libraries, which we'll call the Middle State University Library, with a staff size of 125. However, to broaden our perspective, we'll take occasional side trips to other libraries and even other eras in academic library history.

Arriving at the front entrance, we find our way to the main circulation or checkout desk. It would be nice if we first encountered an information desk, but none is visible. Though I visited a large number of academic libraries while writing this book, I encountered only a handful of public service desks that were staffed by real people (as opposed to automated kiosks) and that were intended to assist customers immediately upon entering the library. Like most academic libraries, Middle State's circulation desk is a vast structure that includes a large number of staff workstations. Only a few of them appear to be in use. Self-checkout stations now satisfy the needs of many customers, and of the staff workstations still in use, most are tenanted by student workers. The library staff directory, however, lists a number of permanent part-time and full-time staff members assigned to the circulation department. "Where are they?" we might ask. Most are probably in the office or workroom behind the desk. They are separated from the public by a wall, whether glass or drywall.

Although I found that permanent circulation staff were completely invisible to the public in many academic libraries, this is not the case at Middle State. A staff member is seated at an office desk positioned in the space between the public counter and the workroom. Although the reason for his presence is to supervise the student workers and solve the weightier problems they encounter, this staff member appears to be immersed in paperwork. He seems to be unaware of most of what is transpiring in the public area. Let us say, however, that we have located one staff member who is visible to the public. What about the other 124 staff members? Let's continue with our explorations.

Reference Then and Now

Even though library literature has been announcing the death of reference for a number of years, most academic libraries still have at least one reference desk. Before we go off in search of the Middle State reference desk, however, let me take you on a side trip back to prehistoric times when I was a very junior public service librarian at Syracuse University. In those days, there was a large reference *room* staffed by perhaps eight reference librarians. In addition, there were three rather large help desks, one on each floor of the terribly inconvenient old Carnegie building. Each help desk was staffed by three librarians and some paraprofessionals. Note that these were in addition to the usual service desks like reserves and interlibrary loan; they did not replace them. I was assigned to the social sciences desk and that was where I spent my time, when I wasn't tracking down wayward volumes on treacherous, glass-floored stack levels. I do not recall that any of us had an office except possibly the head of reference. We assisted customers, selected books, created pathfinders, contributed to the library newsletter, evaluated periodical holdings, and generally did most of the same things that public service staff still do, but we were never out of public view. This meant that although the library was literally crumbling under their feet, students and faculty could always find someone to help them and even accompany them to distant nooks and crannies.

Of course, the number of librarians in most university libraries has dropped sharply, while library floor space has quintupled or sextupled since those days. However, the change that may perhaps be more significant from the customer's perspective is the exodus of today's librarians and other staff members from public areas. Library literature first encouraged "downtime" for reference librarians to allow them to recharge their batteries after the stresses and strains of dealing with the public. For an hour or two a day, they might retreat to a staff-only area and work on their projects without interruption. Soon this meant retreating to their own personal desks and then their own offices or cubicles. Once they got settled in these personal spaces, librarians became reluctant to leave them. They couldn't seem to get anything done when they were working out on "the floor." Their papers, journals, files, and supplies were all stored in their offices.

Soon, "downtime" was seen as time spent working at reference or some other public desk. Concurrently, many academic librarians from other departments were required to take their turn at the reference desk, whether or not they possessed well-developed reference skills. Behind this trend was the theory that librarians with diverse backgrounds could share their expertise with customers. Unfortunately, however, that expertise was not very helpful when it came to advanced search features in "Biological Abstracts." Besides, because reference was not their real job, they came to see these duties as interruptions from their more important work. At about this time, library literature began producing articles about the death of reference. So many reference queries were computer-related or lowly directional questions. Why waste the talents of professional librarians on such mundane matters? Surely paraprofessionals could answer these questions just as well as reference librarians. In fact, paraprofessionals who spent more hours at the reference desk could sometimes provide better answers because they had time to get to know locations and collections.

Where Is Everyone?

This just about brings us back to the present, so let's continue our library tour. We are approaching a long counter identified by a hanging sign that reads "Reference" (or in other libraries "Information"). There are two staff members assigned to the desk, one a librarian and the other a paraprofessional. During peak hours, Middle State may assign a second librarian to the desk whose usual job is not reference. Of course, no two university libraries are alike. Some assign more staff, and others may use library science or other graduate students. During evening and weekend hours, one lone individual may be holding the fort, or the desk may be closed after 8:00 p.m. Nevertheless, let's add three staff members to our count, bringing us to a total of four visible staff members.

Most university libraries have some other public desks. Middle State staffs a document delivery/interlibrary loan desk and a help desk in the information commons area. Other university libraries may also provide a media/audiovisual desk or a separate information desk. Public service desks vary greatly from one library to another, but for the purposes of this exercise, let's assume that our library has two additional public service stations, each staffed by at least one staff member. This is perhaps overly optimistic, because there are many times when customers are served only by student workers. Nevertheless, we will increase our count of visible library staff to six. Wait, you argue. What about the staff members who work evening and weekend hours? In truth, very few permanent staff actually work weekends, but just to be fair, we will assume that half again this number of staff members are scheduled for these hours, bringing the number of visible library staff members to nine. While researching this book, I have taken many tours of university libraries and I often failed to encounter anywhere near this number of staff members.

The Library at Low Ebb

While we are on the subject of evenings and weekends, let's consider the impact of library staffing on part-time students. Class-scheduling practices vary from one college or university to another. However, typical part-time students probably work at full-time jobs and take one or two evening classes. This means that perhaps twice a week, they leave work at 5:00 p.m. and attend a class that begins at 7:00 p.m. Depending on commuting time, it is often impractical to go home after work, so they drive directly to the campus and pick up a quick hamburger at the food court. The best way to use the time that remains is to spend it in the library. Because students often put off class assignments until the last minute, many of these students will be checking out reserve materials, using the Internet, and printing out their homework assignments.

In my experience, library staffing is at low ebb at this time and is almost entirely students. The reason, as you know, is that most full-time staff members work from about 8:30 a.m. to 5:00 p.m., while those working the smaller evening shift are scheduled from about 12:30 to 9:00 p.m. This means that once the lunch hour is over, the library is actually double-staffed until the evening group takes their dinner break and everyone else goes home. By 5:30 or 6:00 p.m., perhaps the only time when nontraditional students can use the library, most of the permanent staff are off duty. Invariably, this is the time when the copy machine runs out of paper or the printer gasps for more toner. Of course, no one on the student staff knows where the key to the storage cabinet is kept, so naturally a crisis ensues. In another frequent scenario, the Internet connection goes down, but technicians work 8:30 to 5:00, Monday through Friday. Even the minimally skilled student technician is taking his break. Besides, he wasn't entrusted with the key to the server room, so he might not be able to solve the problem anyway.

Most academic libraries have few staff members who are actually working in public areas at any time. But during this crucial early evening period, there may be no more than one staff member on whom the entire weight of library services rests. Smaller college libraries may even leave the library entirely in the care of students. On the other hand, most academic institutions have greatly increased the number of nontraditional course offerings, and many professional programs are taught almost entirely in the evening. If half the student body is composed of part-time students, half the student body experiences the library at low ebb. To them, it is little more than a place to sit down, make a few photocopies if the machines don't happen to be out of order, and use the public computers if they are available. There is no one to guide them through the vast stack areas, no one to help them with a difficult database search, and no one to tell them how the library could be of enormous help in meeting their academic needs.

The Customer's Perspective

However, let's get back to the permanent library staff who work at the Middle State University Library. Recall that when we checked the National Center for Education Statistics website, we concluded that a staff size of 100–200 people is fairly typical for a medium-sized university library. Middle State's staff numbers 125, of whom about 116 staff members do not interact with customers during a significant portion of their workweek. Of course, they may repair a computer in a public area, consult with faculty, occasionally telephone library users who have requested interlibrary loans, or even work at a service desk for a few hours when Mary Jones calls in sick. During most of their workday, however, they are unseen by the students, faculty, and other customers who daily use the library.

Now let's imagine students checking the OPAC, wandering through the stacks, printing out journal articles, and generally using the library in the usual ways. As they traverse the acres of stack and study areas, do they encounter many of the *visible* staff members we have identified? Probably not. In fact, the library may be so large that they are only dimly aware of the student workers, who are much more numerous. Many university libraries have installed self-checkout machines so customers may bypass the circulation staff entirely.

If neither students nor faculty encounter real live staff members, they will inevitably view the library as a sort of warehouse. It might be a nice warehouse and they may have generally positive feelings about visiting it, but it is a warehouse nonetheless. As we will be discussing at greater length, public attitudes toward higher education are changing. State legislators and other governing bodies have begun doubting that higher education should be a right of citizens and are demanding that students shoulder a larger part of the cost. Many universities are in constant fear of budget cuts. If you were a university decision maker, would you feel justified in spending scarce funds to pay the salaries of a hundred or more invisible library staff members? Of course, someone has to process the collection and get it on the shelves, but isn't that the job of a warehouse clerk? Is there any reason why warehouse clerks should earn salaries that are in the same ballpark with those of teaching faculty members? From the look of things, students appear to do all the work in the library anyway.

That's not fair, you say? What about all those librarians involved in instruction? They're visible, aren't they? They're obviously professionals, and since teaching is a high-status role in academe, they project a more impressive image. Let's be honest, however. How many hours a day or how many hours a week are such librarians actually interacting with students and faculty? Does the average faculty member spend time working with librarians? Does he or she invite librarians to classes? Although there are indeed some very active information literacy programs, we must admit that most faculty members have little or no interaction with librarians. And if they don't interact with librarians, it's unlikely that their students are active library users.

How Customers See the Library

Remember, however, that we are touring the library building. We have identified several staff members stationed at help desks. Most of these desks are located on the main floor, often in a central service area near the entrance. University libraries, however, are huge—often resembling warehouses in size and perhaps even larger. Warehouses, however, were not intended to be open to the public. No matter whether they are clean, dirty, or color-coordinated, few people are likely to notice or care. On the other hand, students and faculty care a great deal about such things. They form attitudes about the library and the library staff based on what they see. They don't like to use dirty restrooms and they don't enjoy stepping over carpet stains. They rightly assume that it is the responsibility of the library staff—aka warehouse clerks—to maintain a clean, pleasant environment. Bookstores, restaurants, and most of the other places they visit provide such environments. Why not the library?

Imagine the restrooms in our typical medium-sized library. Let's say there are about a dozen of them, five for the use of each sex and maybe a couple of unisex facilities. How many library staff members use these restrooms? In most places, the invisible library staff use equally invisible "staff-only" restrooms. So do the visible library staff unless their service desk is too far distant. Who is responsible for checking public restrooms to be sure they're clean, to make sure soap and paper products are in readiness? The custodial staff? Most library cleaning tends to be done at night. That probably leaves at least sixteen hours each day, as well as the entire weekend, when custodians are not available. I've asked this question to a large number of library directors and library supervisors, and I've concluded that this task is rarely the responsibility of any staff members. More than once, I have been given a name or a job title, only to discover that the staff member so identified has never been informed of this responsibility. One library access services manager responded that she depended on customers to keep her informed. Do you regularly notify the bookstore manager of the condition of the bookstore restroom? Do you feel a responsibility to inspect the restrooms at your favorite restaurant? Of course not! Only if you become angry enough to make a complaint will your opinion be shared.

Responsibility for Public Spaces

The point of this intimate discussion of restrooms is to make it clear that the vast majority of the library staff spend little time in public spaces. They are largely unaware of the condition of the vast public areas and consider them to be someone else's responsibility. The library staff, whether visible or invisible, feel little sense of ownership of the library building. Staff members almost never view themselves as hosts, welcoming the public to their realm. "Yes, that huge carpet stain on the third floor has been there for a year now. Someone definitely ought to do something about it." Who should do something about it? "The custodians, of course!" Who should remind the custodians about it? This question evokes a variety of answers. Perhaps the library director should communicate the problem, but then the library director has far too many responsibilities to become the official carpet inspector. Perhaps public services managers should be responsible, but they too have weighty responsibilities. Perhaps the custodial staff shouldn't have to be told. After all, it's their job, not ours. Possibly not in the best of all possible worlds but in this less-than-perfect world, they obviously must be told.

It seems to me that this sense of being separate and detached from both the library building and library customers is almost unique to the academic library staff. Public libraries have not only survived but prospered amid the extraordinary changes of the last few decades. Book circulation is down in many public libraries, but they have responded by finding new ways to attract local residents. They have lured new customers with both their services and their emphasis on the library as a place, a very nice and inviting place. Technology has impacted and possibly even endangered academic libraries just as it has public libraries. Could it be that a similar response is in order?

IMAGINING THE PERFECT LIBRARY

Now let's stretch our imaginations and visualize a library that doesn't actually exist. Our hypothetical library will be about 125,000 square feet in size. That number may or may not be typical of a medium-sized university library, but it's convenient for this exercise. It will allow us to assign each of our 125 library staff members (both visible and invisible) 1,000 square feet of their very own. In the real world this might be impractical, but let's pursue the possibility in our imaginations and see what could happen. You'll quickly realize how impressed I was with the library I described in the last chapter, the one that found a way to create information desks on every floor. In this imaginary library, we'll take their idea several steps further and see how things develop.

The library director has tried to consider the interests of staff members when making assignments and has encouraged each to feel a special sense of ownership. In other words, each staff member in this imaginary library feels personally responsible for the condition of his or her small plot (a little like a community garden). Although the thought of 125,000 square feet of library space is overwhelming, 1,000 square feet is the size of a small house or apartment. We are all familiar with such a space and accustomed to maintaining it. Staff members in our imaginary library are, in a sense, hosts who ensure that customers have a positive experience when they visit their personal chunks of library real estate.

Imagine that you yourself are responsible for such a space. Maybe you start the workday with a brief visit and stop by for a moment later in the day when you are on your way to a meeting. Perhaps you discover a broken chair leg and initiate a work order. If one custodian usually cleans your area, you get to know each other, either in person or via brief notes, and you share your discoveries. You notice the coffee spill or the walls that need painting.

You discover a pile of books hidden in the corner. Your interior decorating "bump" may even inspire you to change the furniture arrangement or hang some artwork. The space will take on a lived-in, looked-after feel that is completely lacking in most university libraries. The total time spent may amount to no more than ten or fifteen minutes a day, but those few minutes make all the difference. Of course, you'll need to coordinate any changes you make with other staff members. After all, there are no library islands. However, this group is quite different from the bored committee who decided that all carpeting would be gray and all walls a single neutral hue. It's probably not practical to divide the library into thousand-foot chunks, but it is possible to reconnect the library staff with their building.

Moving In

Let's take our imaginary library one step further. Imagine that some of our new landlords are not content to spend a few minutes inspecting their holdings. They are revolutionaries who move their desks out into their public areas. The library director (who is known to be somewhat eccentric) thinks this is an excellent idea. She purchases lockable file cabinets and hardware to secure computer equipment. Electrical and data requirements pose fewer problems than you might expect because wireless access is provided throughout the library. Because customers are encouraged to plug in their laptops, electrical outlets are much more numerous than they were a few years ago. Of course, staff members need telephones. If, for some reason, it proves too inconvenient or expensive to add a number of new telephone jacks, Internet-based telephone services are almost as convenient. Staff need only plug in their headsets to be connected to the world.

Let's imagine once again that you work in this imaginary library. You may continue to lock your valuables in a staff area, but otherwise you have everything you need at your new workstation. If you discover a need for anything else, book trucks are nearby to transport files, journals, or equipment. Of course, it's not as easy to chat with other staff members, but you keep an instant messaging program loaded on your desktop. You can confer with your colleagues about library business or exchange a joke or two. You might even share your online user name with some faculty members or graduate students who need a little extra help.

Very quickly you begin to notice the customers who find their way to your area. When you hear approaching footsteps, you probably look up, make eye contact, and exchange a brief smile. For a number of reasons, this usually doesn't happen when customers approach one of the huge battleships we call service desks. Perhaps their height is intimidating, or staff members are busy with other customers. Then again, staff may appear to be hiding behind the desk, because most of their bodies are concealed. A lone individual behind a standard office desk appears much more exposed and vulnerable, and so it seems natural to exchange greetings. After a week or so, you begin to notice the same customers returning. We are all uncomfortable in strange places, and most of us are creatures of habit. Customers tend to choose the same table or the same study carrel whenever it is available. They may also be taking courses that make use of the collection materials shelved in your area. Soon you begin recognizing faces and students recognize you. When they have questions, they are more likely to bring them to you than to the forbidding presence at the service desk downstairs. Although you are not a reference librarian, you begin to know your area intimately. You can access the OPAC from your desktop, and you can send off a quick message to a more appropriate staff member.

Professional and Paraprofessional Roles

Of course, it is uncomfortable to talk with someone who is looming above you, so you borrow a couple of chairs to place beside your new desk. Now you can actually have conversations with students and faculty. Again, this is something that is difficult at large service desks but is an extremely impor-tant part of the information-seeking process. Oops! Doesn't this mean that any staff member who moves his or her desk out into a public area is going to be conducting reference interviews? Yes, it does. It means that both stu-dents and faculty will choose library representatives who wouldn't normally be involved in such activities. If we value these relationships, these personal interactions that would not otherwise occur, then we have an obligation to support them.

Why should we demand that customers descend two flights of stairs to consult the reference librarian when an intermediary can get them to-gether electronically? Working as a team, staff member and reference li-brarian can combine forces to quickly satisfy their customer's information need. Helping staff members become more aware of their own limitations and the strengths of their colleagues is, therefore, essential in this brave new library world and this, in turn, brings up a particular grievance of mine. For all the years that I have been a librarian, our profession has reprimanded support staff who dared to venture into what we considered our bailiwick; in other words, to answer reference questions. In effect, we told support staff that they were not educated enough or skilled enough to respond to these intellectual queries and should limit themselves to directing customers to the restrooms. Then, after convincing everyone of the vitally important role of the reference librarian, we downsized reference services.

Although this kind of professional territorialism is almost never in the best interest of our customers, it is certainly true that sophisticated reference skills can save customers a great deal of time and frustration. Is it so very difficult to teach a staff member to view the reference librarian as a partner, a colleague who is there to offer help when help is needed? Obviously, staff members want their customers' information needs to be met and are intelligent enough to choose the quickest and best way to meet those needs, whether they rely upon their own expertise or get help from colleagues.

Combining Public Service with Other Duties

However, you've been sitting at your imaginary desk during this outburst and you have a lot of work to do. How will you get it done if you are spending your time assisting the public? To answer this question, you might take a good look at your library's stack and study areas. Except during peak periods, most of the library is not heavily used. In fact, there are usually large areas that are almost empty of customers. The number of students and faculty who will occupy your time with their questions or their company is actually not very great. Most of your time will continue to be spent performing the other duties in your job description.

Of course, once you place yourself and your desk in the midst of such empty spaces, they may not remain empty. That's because many customers, especially women students, feel uncomfortable studying where no other human being is in sight. In the case of tower-type libraries, there may be no one else on the entire floor. Haven't you been in this situation? You find yourself in some distant corner of your library and you begin to feel ill at ease. You wonder whether anyone would hear you if you screamed. You hear a noise and imagine that someone is lurking in the stacks. Of course, there are people who deliberately seek out such spaces, but most of us are just a little cowardly. We're comforted by the presence of a staff member nearby and with good reason. Staff can telephone for help or press a panic button to signal an emergency. Besides, you as a staff member are viewed as a symbol of authority, someone who can maintain order or deal with a crisis. What? The Internet goes down? You can page a technician. A toilet overflows? You summon a custodian.

But I see you still have reservations. How is it possible to supervise a staff that is dispersed throughout the library? Won't some take advantage of the situation to play solitaire and purchase their spring wardrobes online? Yes, indeed! However, many businesses are faced with the same problem. Good management and supervisory skills become even more important in such a library, and measurable goals and objectives are essential. Even so, there are some staff members who might not adjust well to such an unstructured environment, and student workers often require closer supervision. That still leaves a large number of staff members who can get their work done while radically altering the experience of the library's customers.

Balancing Staff Preferences and Library Needs

Earlier in this chapter when I was meandering down memory lane, I mentioned reference librarians who once spent eight hours a day interacting with customers. They quite reasonably demanded an hour or two away from the madding crowd, but more recently their schedules have been turned upside down. Despite the fact that they are still classified as public service or reference librarians, they spend very little time with the public. I think we have to assume that this is their preference. In researching this book, I have collected the job descriptions of a large number of academic librarians. Most of the duties described require a computer. The needed files and software programs can be made available at any library workstation. A few tasks require a high level of concentration that can't be achieved with frequent interruptions, but this is not the norm with most library work.

Reference librarians are certainly not the only staff members who seem to deliberately avoid library customers. If you don't believe this is the case, spend a little time observing behaviors at almost any library service desk. If an office or work area adjoins a service desk, staff will tend to seek it out. Supervisors must enforce formal desk schedules and occasionally roust out resistant staff members when it is discovered that no one is tending to the public desk. Recently, I was watching a very "cheesy" black-and-white film produced in 1947 that was intended to interest high school students in library work. As the camera panned across range after range of books, the narrator asked if viewers thought of books as their friends. "You do? That's wonderful!" I was rolling my eyes as the camera moved on to a stereotypical white-haired librarian surrounded by smiling students. But then the narrator surprised me. "Do you like people too? Wonderful! If you like both books and people, a library career may be right for you." True, this film was not *Gone with the Wind* or *Citizen Kane*, but even in 1947 the library educators responsible for the ideas in the film were on the right track. How is it that our profession has been stressing the importance of people skills all these years, but we organize the library staff in such a way that they have minimal interaction with our customers? How can it be that librarians and other staff members who receive excellent evaluations continually find reasons to avoid the public?

Reinforcing Our Commitment

If we were to examine the textbooks used in library science courses, we would find a plethora of references to user needs. For example, modern cataloging texts are interested in the way that library users search for materials. In fact, every area of library science at least gives lip service to that mission so well enunciated by the patron saint of LIS faculty, S. R. Ranganathan (remember the Five Laws of Library Science: every book its reader; save the time of the reader, etc.?).[1] Most library staff members share this philosophy, so why then do we have this disconnect between the ideal and the reality? It seems to me we have a twofold job ahead of us if we are to transform academic libraries into the customer-centered places we want them to be. On the one hand, we must make sure that the people we are hiring to staff our libraries do indeed enjoy spending time with our customers. Few library staff members are really antisocial, however, and most get a lot of satisfaction out of helping others. What may be missing is an environment in which public service staff can be comfortable and productive. We may be failing to create a structure that allows staff members to feel at ease in public areas.

To illustrate what I mean, let's take another field trip and look in on a real-world library. Look over there at that staff member who is scheduled to work at a public desk. He or she might be a paraprofessional who is assigned occasionally to the information desk, or an access services clerk who is scheduled on the circulation desk when he is not sending out overdue notices in the staff work area. But since we've been talking about the fate of reference, let's focus on this area. We'll tag along behind a librarian who is on the reference desk schedule today and will shortly be starting a two-hour shift. She is now in her office or cubicle, working on a committee report that contains some particularly thorny recommendations. When she notices the clock, she groans. What a bad time to interrupt this important project!

Oh well, duty calls. She picks up a pen and a copy of *Choice* and, somewhat resentfully, goes out to the reference desk. In this case it's a tall, bank-type counter, a smaller version of the circulation desk. She may choose either to stand behind the desk or to sit on a high stool that becomes uncomfortable after half an hour. Typically, the staff side of the desk contains a few drawers intended for pencils, pens, and other small objects, as well as several open shelves. No personal belongings are ever kept there. If library offices are on a different floor or otherwise far distant from the reference desk, librarians feel they are journeying to a primitive land. They dare not bring their purses or briefcases because there are no locked drawers to secure them. Their favorite pens are likely to be left behind, so they make do with pencils. Similarly, keys, aspirin, lipstick, or breath mints may be forgotten, so librarians feel stranded without the small possessions that bring them comfort. Even a water bottle may be frowned upon. Librarians rarely attempt to continue with the tasks they were working on because their books and files clutter the desk surface. In fact, librarians even feel uncomfortable loading their own files on the reference computer because the OPAC and the university's portal to online databases must be ever at the ready. Is it any wonder that librarians dread reference duty?

I have a friend who once worked briefly at an America Online call center. Because the center operated twenty-four hours a day, three shifts of employees occupied the work space. Management fought a never-ending battle to prevent staff from "nesting" at their workstations. To be comfortable at work, most human beings need to make a "nest." They need to have a space that is in some way personal and familiar. That means photos of family members, birthday cards, joke gifts, and perhaps a potted plant on their desks. They also need personal items like ChapStick, gum, and safety pins to deal with discomfort and small emergencies. To accommodate these needs, America Online provided lockers and encouraged staff to bring all personal items to their lockers at the end of their shifts. Nevertheless, desks invariably sprouted Mickey Mouse pen holders, baby photos, and humorous nameplates.

However, we have strayed from the librarian perched awkwardly behind the reference desk. How would things be different if she worked in the imaginary library described above? To answer that question, we'll move her out of her office to a small desk in a public area on the second floor, situated amid study tables and book stacks. Actually, it is her old desk, which still holds her nail file, her cough drops, and her water bottle. Behind her is a lateral file cabinet that contains her miscellaneous paperwork, review journals, and the other items she needs to do her job effectively. All drawers can be locked when she leaves the area. If another staff member occupies the space in the evenings, a second desk is added. With the help of a telephone and access to the library's computer network, the librarian is able to carry out her old responsibilities.

After she's become accustomed to her new surroundings, other changes will gradually begin occurring. She places a sign on her desk that reads

"Interrupt me," and many students take advantage of the invitation. For example, John, a student writing his master's thesis in political science, begins stopping by her desk almost every day. Since discovering his "friendly neighborhood librarian," John is progressing more rapidly on his thesis and he's found an area in the library where he feels at home, where he too can nest. Similarly, a new freshman stumbled upon this staff workstation when she needed a campus map and now thinks of the librarian as a safe port in the storm of unfamiliar campus life. Other students have gravitated to the area as well. Because they're getting to know the librarian, they feel comfortable reporting problems like graffiti in the restroom. However, since it is now more convenient for the librarian herself to use that same public restroom, she has already notified the custodian.

You might think that all this public exposure is uncomfortable for the librarian, but she's actually happier than she ever was in her old library. She rarely got to know her customers at that big, uncomfortable reference desk. In fact, most of her contacts were with library staff members, and she knew few students or faculty personally. Now she knows what's going on around campus. When John and other graduate students submit their research projects, her name figures prominently in the acknowledgment section, where she is thanked for her invaluable help. Maybe this doesn't seem like such a "big deal," but it really matters. We need to know that what we do is important. Because many other staff members have desks in public areas, no one librarian or paraprofessional is overburdened with questions, but the overall number of customer encounters is growing rapidly.

Real versus Imaginary Libraries

Of course, real libraries are more complex and more difficult to administer than our imaginary one. They bring together a wide variety of personalities, customer needs, bureaucratic requirements, and, inevitably, problems. It is not possible to wave a magic wand and create the delightful environment described in this chapter. Nevertheless, we can't continue to accept a system that we know is not working. There seems to be no question that real-world, nonvirtual libraries are in trouble. Most of us are continuing to see the decline in library usage that Scott Carlson described in 2001.[2] On the other hand, libraries that are bucking the trend, those developing new strategies to attract customers, are succeeding. There seems to be little question that there are roles that academic libraries can play that are consistent with their missions and that will attract new customers. It has become extremely important that we sit down, put on our thinking caps, and discover what they are.

NOTES

1. S. R. Ranganathan, *The Five Laws of Library Science* (London: Blunt and Sons, 1957).
2. Scott Carlson, "The Deserted Library: As Students Work Online, Reading Rooms Empty Out—Leading Some Campuses to Add Starbucks," *Chronicle of Higher Education,* November 16, 2001, A35; available at http://chronicle.com/free/v48/i12/12a03501.htm.

RESOURCES

Miller, Rush. "What Difference Do We Make?" *Journal of Academic Librarianship* 33, no. 1 (January 2007): 1–2.

Rooks, D. C. "You Gotta Believe!" *Journal of Academic Librarianship* 32, no. 6 (November 2006): 646–47.

Sauer, J. L. "Developing Academic Library Staff for Future Success." *Journal of Academic Librarianship* 31, no. 2 (March 2005): 168.

Tennant, Roy. "Academic Library Futures." *Library Journal* 131, no. 20 (December 2006): 34.

4

A GREAT PLACE TO BE

Creating a Livable Library

As the academic community discovers that it can access many of the resources it needs from home, its members may begin to wonder whether they really need brick-and-mortar academic libraries. Public libraries are also struggling in the digital era, but they have discovered a truth that may not be widely understood in the academic library community. Public librarians have learned that their customers come to the library, at least in part, to have an experience. They come for the pleasure of curling up with an enjoyable book, getting out of the house, and seeing their friends and neighbors. A library visit can be a brief respite from an otherwise stressful day, a pleasant interlude in an agreeable, entertaining, and attractive environment. Academic libraries can become just such places without sacrificing their scholarly priorities.

A BELONGING PLACE

Faculty members are entitled to personal spaces on campus, so they are not often seen in the library. Students, on the other hand, are in a sense "homeless." Commuters may be required to spend much of their day on campus and they need a place to relax, study, and generally pull themselves together between classes. Dorms are often noisy and unpleasant places that resident students prefer to avoid. What kind of place do students prefer?

Today's students have grown up in a different world from their parents and have different expectations. For example, some students may still need a quiet environment in which to study, but others are far more comfortable when they are surrounded by sound. Can we take these individual differences into consideration and provide for a variety of different noise levels? Some look for a "nest," where they can feel as if they're in their own small space. This means they will avoid huge study spaces where tables and study carrels march like soldiers in long, straight lines. Although a few students seek out the most remote and uninhabited reaches of a library, most settle down in areas where they can see other students nearby. Each of us has a slightly different attitude toward the space around us, and these attitudes may change as our needs change. If we have a paper due tomorrow, we will see the library much differently than if we simply want to get out of our dorm rooms and work on an assignment in the company of our fellow students.

Personalizing Library Space

In the course of my research, I visited a very large and well-funded university library that was recently renovated and enlarged. Vast acreages of open library space confront the user on every floor. All are precisely the same hue, probably chosen by a decorator because it was an "in" color. Because it was such a popular color, the decorator was able to match walls, carpet, and furniture to the exact shade. The furnishings were also identical in design. For example, one chair design had been chosen for use with all study carrels and tables. Because this was a very large library, perhaps a thousand copies in exactly the same size and style were purchased. Apparently, it never entered anyone's mind that customers come in different shapes and sizes. A chair that is comfortable for a small woman is probably very uncomfortable for a large man. Students with back problems or athletic injuries may prefer a hard, straight-backed chair, while most others appreciate some cushioning. (At another library, I found a sea of wooden chairs with absolutely no padding. Many people can sit on such chairs for less than half an hour before becoming uncomfortable.) Because walls are few (partitions make supervision difficult in a library), the impression this huge, monochrome library creates is a boring blur, with only book stacks emerging from the uninviting and unexciting environment.

Apart from the problem that everyone will be thoroughly sick of the trendy color in just a few years, the library has lost the opportunity to reach out and meet the individual needs of its customers. Every area is identical to every other area. Unless there is a functional necessity to separate a section, like a computer lab or multimedia area, nothing interrupts the seemingly endless monochrome spaces. Nothing attracts the eye; no comfy nook beckons. Despite luxurious, deep-pile carpeting and color-coordinated lounge furniture placed here and there, nothing says "Come, curl up with a book or magazine, and just enjoy being here."

As I mentioned, this is a vast library that can accommodate thousands of customers, but each of those customers will have an experience that is identical to all the others. No effort has been made to accommodate personal preferences; no attempt has been made to consider individual needs. If students and other customers don't happen to like the color or the ambience, then too bad. If the chairs are so high that their feet don't reach the ground, or the carrels are too small to accommodate both books and laptops, they have two options. They can remain and make do with discomfort, or they can leave.

Library 2.0

Customers have certainly not left this library in droves, but neither have they been strongly attracted to it. On a typical day when classes are being held, most of the available seats are vacant. Perhaps the thick carpet silences footsteps and intensifies the impression of a vast, vacant space, but nevertheless that impression is well founded. When one thinks of the financial resources that were available for this project, one can imagine all sorts of inviting spaces. There was plenty of space and sufficient money to design a library that really met the needs of a wide variety of customers. What a marvelous opportunity to design a library around the real, twenty-first-century needs of students and faculty! As discussed earlier, Library 2.0 represents a philosophy of library service that has been sweeping the academic library community. At the core of Library 2.0 is the belief that to prosper, libraries must partner with their customers to rethink the whole notion of the academic library. Customers must be involved in the planning process to a degree that was never considered necessary in the past. Unless customers tell us what they need and then become intimately involved in the development of services to meet those needs, we cannot expect to prosper in the twenty-first century.

So let's get back to this one-size-fits-all library. It appears that library planners, both design professionals and librarians, imagined one hypothetical or generic user, because every piece of furniture in this library and every decorative element is equally generic. ADA requirements were met, but what about the requirements of real, nongeneric students, each of whom has unique needs and preferences? Of course, it is not possible to purchase a thousand different chair styles to meet the needs of a thousand different students, but it is possible to begin with a reasonably large number of bona fide students who are at least somewhat representative of their peers and find out what matters to them. Each student may be unique, but patterns do emerge.

THE CUSTOMER'S-EYE VIEW

To illustrate some ways in which student needs can guide library planning, I'm going to describe some students I have worked with in the past, whose personal and academic lives to some extent typify students who can be found at your college or university. These are not generic students since I am "drawing them from life." However, they are not your students either. Their experience of the library may provide a starting point, but there is no substitute for partnering with the students attending your own academic institution. Because advanced students use the library very differently from beginning students, I've chosen a traditional, full-time freshman, a non-traditional, part-time master's student, and a Ph.D. student preparing for comps (or quals, depending on your institutional jargon).

Once again, I've returned to the world of the imagination and placed these students in a near-perfect library. This time, however, my library is not completely imaginary. I've taken elements from the best libraries I visited and merged them into one wonderful library. Even some struggling libraries beset by budget crises and other depressing problems have often managed to create very livable, workable spaces. The secret of their success was that despite the problems they were experiencing, they continued to communicate with their customers. Not only were students frequently consulted about their likes and dislikes, but staff observed which areas were sought out and which were avoided, which chairs were in use and which gathered dust.

AN UNDERGRADUATE'S EXPERIENCE

Justin is an undergraduate at a large state university. His dorm is on the periphery of the campus, and his car is parked in a university lot that is even more remote. Although he gets along well with his roommate, they do not share the same taste in music, and their room is often noisy and occupied by both his roommate and his roommate's friends. Justin walks or takes the shuttle to the central campus just before his first class. He tends to remain in this central area the remainder of the day. Most of his classes are here, as well as the dining hall, the food court, his part-time job in the student center, and, of course, the main university library. Over the course of the day, Justin has several free hours. Now, let's give him a library that exactly meets his needs, a library that Justin would design if he had our knowledge of libraries and the expertise of our architects.

Justin is coming to the library directly from class. Because the day is dark, cold, and brooding, Justin is looking for a warm place to study and just pass the time before his next class. It's always something of a relief when his first class is over, and Justin needs to unwind now. He heads first for the conveniently located restroom that's only a short distance from the library's main entrance. Because its location makes this one of the most heavily used restrooms in the library, it is thoroughly cleaned several times a day. Although other restrooms may not be cleaned as often, all are checked regularly, so the towel, toilet paper, and liquid soap dispensers are refilled as needed (I told you this was a fantasy).

Still not ready to settle down to study, Justin decides that a cup of well-caffeinated coffee will make him more alert. Of course, our imaginary library has an inviting café, also located off the lobby. It is attractively decorated like a Starbucks or Barnes and Noble and offers quality food and beverages. Justin's café is not hidden in the basement with poor lighting, and it's not just a rank of coin-operated machines that dispense junk food and an undrinkable liquid misnamed coffee. The tables are cleared and wiped off regularly, and Justin can set his backpack on the floor, knowing it will not be coated with sticky goop when he retrieves it. A pleasant leisure reading area is also located off the lobby and adjacent to the café. Justin can pick out a magazine or a sci-fi thriller to read while he sips his espresso without fear that he is breaking any library rules. Most of us would consider this a near-perfect break from the day's toil, and Justin is not the only one who would appreciate it.

We sometimes forget that the library has a big advantage when it comes to attracting students. If you were to talk with some of them—and I don't mean just the students who regularly hang out with us—you would discover that their superegos highly approve of the library. In other words, their voice of conscience may be saying, "I should go to the library and study for my test," or "I should go to the library and get a head start on that homework assignment." At the same time, their less virtuous selves want to "chill out" and focus on creature comforts. Justin has just spent the last twenty minutes reveling in comfort with nary a twinge from his conscience. After all, he's getting ready to work. He's settling down, reviving his energies—whatever he wants to call it—but it's very pleasant, and the library gets all the credit.

A Place to Be Productive

Now it's time for Justin to tear himself away from his sci-fi reading and find a place where he can work on that homework assignment for political science. Of course, our fantasy library has a great information commons equipped with up-to-date hardware and software that never crashes or loses the library's well-maintained network connection. However, it tends to be crowded, and Justin wants to get off by himself and find a place where he won't be distracted. He also wants to be near the poly sci books, because he expects to need them. On the second floor, he finds the perfect spot with a good-size table and comfortable chair. Since he will need his laptop computer, text, notebook, and possibly several library books, he would find most of the study carrels in academic libraries too small for his needs. However, our fantasy library offers enough variety that most students can find a size that works.

Accommodating Laptop Computers

Many academic libraries resemble our fantasy library in that they offer buildingwide wireless connectivity. Students can connect to the library OPAC, the premium journal databases, and the global Internet from anywhere in the library. What makes our fantasy library different, however, is that library planners have actually observed real students and have discussed their computing needs with them. Laptop batteries lose their electrical charge very rapidly, and students rarely arrive at the library with a fully charged battery. Justin plans to remain in the library for a few hours. Because he took class notes on his computer earlier this morning, he needs to plug in and recharge. That means he must have an electrical outlet within a few feet of his table.

As I mentioned earlier, I toured a great many academic libraries while I was gathering information for this book. Among them, I found many recently renovated buildings and even a few brand-new, ultramodern structures. What I did not find were electrical outlets. Even in state-of-the-art information commons facilities boasting excellent computers and the most sophisticated software, I often found students clustered around the half dozen outlets provided for their use. I have no way of knowing how many students bring their laptops to campus with them, but I feel quite sure that the number is a large one. This means that the number of students in Justin's situation is similarly large. Just the ability to find someplace comfortable to sit, plug in their computers, and check their e-mail would mean a great deal to many students, and it is not a very difficult service to provide. Twenty-first-century students have substituted personal computers for paper and pen. They may take class notes in longhand if their instructor objects to the clicking of keys. Otherwise, their academic life resides on their computers. Being unable to use their computers while on campus is like losing the use of an arm or a leg.

The electrical rewiring needed to equip large areas of the library with outlets is, of course, costly. However, most libraries have embarked upon a number of expensive projects to bring technology into the library. I have a feeling that the absence of these outlets is another indication of the failure to allow students and other library customers to participate in the planning process. From the library staff's point of view, it is the library's resources that are important, and expenditures intended to expand and deliver those resources are assumed to be necessary. However, once the library has provided the technology needed to access its online indexes and digital materials, it has done its job. This isn't the way our customers view the situation.

A Twenty-First-Century View of Technology

The planners of our fantasy library understood that the library's technology had to dovetail with Justin's own personal technology to effectively serve his needs. In many libraries, it seems that librarians are trapped in 1980, imagining that students will want to print out journal articles, carry around reams of paper, take notes with pencil and paper, and, finally, type up their assignments or research papers on a library computer. In other words, librarians still view computers as intelligent typewriters. In reality, today's students may never use a sheet of paper until the final printout. Information must flow seamlessly among the computers they will be using, possibly including two or more library desktop computers, a personal laptop, and another desktop computer at home. If Justin is able to recharge his laptop from a convenient AC outlet, his task becomes much simpler. He can remain in the library much longer, and he needn't go through the cumbersome process of exporting data from the library's desktops to his own computer.

Focus on Comfort

After an hour or so, Justin's attention starts to wander. He's beginning to feel uncomfortable, since he's been sitting in one position for so long. He shifts positions in his seat, and his mind shifts to more appealing subjects. We all know this feeling, but younger, less experienced students may have even more difficulty remaining focused on an assignment. Because they are usually taking a full schedule of core courses that are unrelated to their majors, they are likely to find them less interesting than upper-division courses they choose for themselves. Justin may want to move to another area of the library for a change of scene. Our fantasy library offers a wide variety of spaces, and each has an ambience of its own. Remember the monochrome library described above? Every area was identical to every other area. Justin might have been studying on the first floor or the third, but he would scarcely be aware of the difference.

In our fantasy library, spaces have been created with a lot of thought given to individual differences. A tall basketball player, Justin often has trouble finding room for his knees. I myself am near the other end of the spectrum at five feet, three inches. I recently visited a library that had a large number of attractive, recently purchased lounge chairs. All were identical to one another and all were very square-looking, with padded arms at the same height as the padded back. In other words, the chair completely encased its occupant on three sides. Although I am of average weight, I found the chair seat so narrow that when I sat down, I was squeezed into a constricted space, with padding pressing against me on all sides, making it impossible to rise without difficulty. Even though the chair appeared to be made for someone under a hundred pounds, the seat was so high that my feet did not touch the ground. Hence, I struggled to release myself, wriggling first one way and then another until I could plant my feet on the ground and get some leverage. Because the chair's arms were actually sides of the square at the same height as the back, I found that I could not even move my own arms. They were squashed at my side, forcing me to thrust them painfully over my head to free them.

It is obvious that none of the library's planners ever sat in this chair. None but a six-foot-tall individual who weighed less than a hundred pounds would have found it comfortable. The chair was very attractive, however, and precisely matched the library's color scheme, which is probably the reason why it was chosen. It is possible that no one on the library staff actually chose the chair. It may have been the interior designer's choice, and a library administrator simply signed off on a list of furniture selections. I do not mean to imply, however, that all would be well if a few librarians had made it their business to sit on the chairs under consideration. Librarians do not really represent their customers in this respect. They tend to be older than traditional students and have very different needs. They might, for example, have chosen a hard, straight-backed wooden chair because it is good for their sacroiliac. Once again, it is clear that the customers for whom the library is designed must have a voice in such decisions.

Let There Be Light

However, I have wandered away from Justin and his near-perfect library. Remember that outside the library, the day is cold and dark. No sunshine warms the campus, and so the library's window areas seem cold and uninviting. Note that our fantasy library has a lot of windows, since these areas are usually the most popular choices. Customers like to bask in sunshine and see what's going on outside the library. On ugly days like this one, however, they desert the window areas and look for comfy nooks that feel warm and inviting. Our imaginary librarians were aware of this phenomenon and planned accordingly.

At first the planning group wondered how to treat the lower floor of the library that is partly below ground level. Instead of just wondering, however, they visited a number of libraries to see which subterranean, windowless areas were used more heavily. It should be no surprise that lighting was the most significant variable. In some libraries, customers gravitated toward areas where full-spectrum lighting fixtures effectively simulated natural daylight. In others, they sought out study tables where the coziness of incandescent lamps illuminated just the immediate surroundings with a warm, inviting glow. (The new low-energy fluorescent bulbs can simulate a wide variety of lighting conditions, including golden lamplight.) Naturally, this being a fantasy library, the planners decided to provide for both customer preferences.

Since the library had, of course, been generously wired to power laptop computers, table lamps were easily accommodated. As your colleagues can probably tell you, something magical happens when you add table lamps to an uninviting area. Customers are drawn to the lamps like moths! In our fantasy library, the cozy atmosphere created by the lamps is enhanced with a decor designed especially for days like this. The walls are darker and deeper in color; rich, warm hues have been deliberately selected for the carpet and furnishings. Brightly colored posters complete the picture and totally banish the basement look that characterizes the lower levels of so many libraries.

Controlling Sound

Justin finds his way to a table in just such a seating area. This chair is a different shape from the last one he sat on, and the resulting change in posture will add an hour or more of comfort to his library visit. The pleasant lamplight makes reading more enjoyable, and Justin is feeling that cozy, snuggly sense of warmth that we all seek on cold, dark days. In the background, Justin is only vaguely aware of what might be called white noise, the quiet, steady sound of the ventilation system keeping the entire library at a comfortable temperature. There are no crashes or bangs when the system starts up or shuts down. Nor are there any noisy exposed air ducts above Justin's head. Leaving heating ducts and water pipes exposed has become trendy in recent years. In older buildings, necessity has become the mother of invention, and even upscale restaurants often paint their old pipes the same color as the ceiling and consider them part of the decor. Unfortunately, this does not work well in libraries because of the inevitable racket created by air handlers and banging, gurgling water pipes. Our fantasy library planning team insisted that the ventilation system's subcontractor consider the library's special needs by using sound-muffling materials and devices.

THE NONTRADITIONAL STUDENT AND THE LIBRARY

Well, Justin seems to be settling down nicely, so let's fast-forward the clock in our fantasy library to early evening, 5:30 p.m. to be exact. We'll turn our attention from Justin to Marian, a married woman with school-age children, who is working toward a master's degree in business administration. Marian leaves work at 5:00 p.m. and drives straight to the campus. Her main reason for arriving early is to get one of the coveted parking spaces, but she also appreciates the opportunity to spend an extra hour in the library. Years ago when she was an undergraduate, Marian used her college library only very occasionally, and she has since forgotten the little she learned about library research. At work, she uses her desktop computer for e-mail and word processing, but that's the extent of her computer skills.

The Growth of Evening and Weekend Programs

Like so many universities, our library's parent institution has discovered that master's degree programs aimed at nontraditional students are a lucrative source of income. They tend to be inexpensive to operate, since they are usually staffed by low-paid adjunct faculty and rarely require expensive lab facilities. Many employers offer financial incentives to their employees to upgrade their skills. In fact, a master's degree may mean an automatic pay raise. The problem is that such programs force working people to burn the candle at both ends. If they already have families and full-time jobs, they are likely to become stressed out and exhausted. Learning ceases to be a pleasure, and each assignment is viewed as a hurdle in an obstacle course.

Although the number of these graduate programs has been skyrocketing, many academic libraries have done little to accommodate them. Students like Marian who use the library after 5:00 p.m. may encounter a closed interlibrary loan desk, inexperienced student workers struggling to find missing reserve materials, and generally a library that is at low ebb. After a few unpleasant experiences, nontraditional students may come to view the library as one of their more unpleasant hurdles, avoiding it whenever possible.

Meeting the Needs of Invisible Students

Remember, however, that Marian need not endure such a dysfunctional library. She has just entered our fantasy facility, and a totally different kind of experience awaits her. The planning group that designed the library was fully aware of the many nontraditional graduate students it serves and found many creative ways to solicit their input. Although nontraditional students are busier and more rushed than their younger peers, the planners were able to get together a small focus group of students who provided a wealth of ideas. From their comments, planners developed a brief, clearly worded questionnaire that required only a few minutes to complete. Then the problem was how to contact a representative number of such potential customers. Most are shadowy, almost invisible students who hurry directly to their classroom buildings at 7:00 p.m. and depart quickly at 9:30, after most people have left the campus. Because they are so elusive, we have few opportunities to get to know them individually.

However, the university made it easy to identify nontraditional grad students by scheduling most of their classes at precisely 7:00 p.m. This meant that members of the planning team knew when and where to find them. They set up tables in classroom buildings between 6:30 and 7:00 and returned during the period when classes were most likely to take a break. Library planners explained that they were committed to meeting the needs of nontraditional students, and so these students' input was essential. In addition, the planners encouraged adjunct faculty members to take just a few minutes of class time to distribute the questionnaires. This, of course, meant that they had to get to know adjunct faculty members as well, and they were amazed to discover how their needs too had been ignored.

Although the questionnaires resulted in a variety of discoveries about this group of customers and potential customers, the most important findings can be boiled down to two closely related points. First, these students do have assignments that require access to library materials and services, but they often lack even basic library research skills. Many have been out of school for ten or even twenty years. Middle-aged workers may decide to go back to school when they feel their skills are out-of-date and they are being passed over for promotions. Academic libraries have undergone extraordinary changes in the last twenty years, and returning students may find them almost unrecognizable.

Tired, Hungry, and Needing Help

The second thing the planners learned was that nontraditional students arrive on campus stressed, hungry, tired, and cranky. They look on the bureaucratic nightmare that is typical of so many university campuses as the last straw, the one that breaks the camel's back. They began the day hunting for Jimmy's socks, making Suzie's school lunch, and dropping Lisa off at preschool. Then they worked a stressful day, contended with rush hour traffic, and are now facing a long evening class for which they may be unprepared. A library abandoned at 5:00 by most of its staff is seen as part of this nightmare experience, not a haven but an additional burden.

When library planners combined these two discoveries, they began to get a clear picture of Marian and her fellow students. Because they arrived on campus harried and hungry, they needed food, caffeine, and comfortable chairs. But they also needed a well-trained library staff who could work with them individually, accurately assessing their skill levels, considering their time constraints, and custom-tailoring library expertise just for them. Marian, therefore, seeks out the library as a place where she can satisfy her most pressing needs. Like Justin, she begins her visit by stopping at the restroom. She can wash off some of the grime of the day, refresh her makeup, and even change her laddered pantyhose. Even at this late hour, the restroom is clean since it has been checked and order restored several times during the course of the day. There are no burned-out bulbs or flickering fluorescent lights, so she can see herself clearly in the large mirror. She can brush the cat hair from her sweater and make herself presentable for the long evening ahead.

Food in the Library

Now Marian needs a place where she can both study and eat. This means that the café is open and will remain available to students until after the break that usually occurs at about the midpoint of evening classes. When Marian was taking a concentrated weekend course, she found that most campus eating places were closed, but the café was open during the most popular hours. But perhaps Marian picked up a hamburger on her way to the library. She wants to find a quiet reading area away from the hubbub of the café, eat her hamburger, and study for her quiz. This means that the library needs to have additional areas where food and drink are permitted. Library planners did their homework well, and they discovered that it's not really so difficult to accommodate food and drink in academic libraries as was once believed.

It requires a clear understanding of the nature of the library's collections, however. In general, effective custodial services allow many library materials to coexist with a more lenient policy, but special collections and other resources intended to be retained for long periods of time should be shelved on upper levels where stricter rules prevail.

Evening and Weekend Staffing

Because our fantasy library is adequately staffed during the early evening hours, Marian has no difficulty checking out reserve materials, using the library OPAC, or picking up an interlibrary loan request. However, her course requires a substantial final project, and Marian has not done any academic writing or research for nearly twenty years. She needs a lot more than a friendly circulation clerk to acquire the skills she needs. Although she is a graduate student and brings with her a wealth of experience in the business world, she is lacking basic research skills. Even when reference librarians in real-world libraries are available to help students like Marian, the encounter may be unpleasant. Students may be feeling defensive, determined to be treated as adults, not as ignorant freshmen. Experience with the university bureaucracy may put them automatically on their guard, braced for yet another negative exchange. Librarians may feel that such students treat them as they might treat shoe store clerks, demanding instant answers and materials placed in their hands with little effort on their part.

Naturally, our fantasy librarians are aware of these potential land mines. They understand that nontraditional grad students have been placed in a sort of catch-22 situation. On the one hand, the university admissions staff actively courts students like Marian, encouraging them to believe that they can work full-time and still earn a graduate degree in a very short time. On the other hand, the university faculty wants its graduate degrees to be viewed with respect, not seen as the products of diploma mills. So Marian and her peers are caught in the middle, with too little time to complete their assignments in the way that is expected of them. University librarians too are caught in the middle. They want to make these nontraditional students happy, but they also believe that learning research methods should be part of almost any graduate program.

Establishing Relationships with Nontraditional Students

As mentioned earlier, the planners of our fantasy library put a lot of work into analyzing and responding to the needs of this group of customers. They learned that nontraditional graduate students may feel very out of place on campus. They're outsiders and they don't spend enough time at their university to know the ropes. Naturally, our fantasy library boasts an exceptionally effective information desk located near the main entrance. Information desk staff installed a large, colorful sign intended specifically to attract nontraditional students. Then they added a literature rack that contains brochures and flyers just for this group, and the library website offers similar materials. Their first goal was to attract these students, to convince them that the library could be their home away from home and the source of needed information. At the library, they could get not only the usual campus maps but insider recommendations about campus parking, food, drink, and even campus restrooms. These are not the dry, official publications the university produces. They contain personalized tips culled from the suggestions of experienced traditional students. Because the library café is one of the few food service facilities that remain open during evening hours, nontraditional students pass by the information desk frequently on their way to the café.

The information desk staff are taught to skillfully steer students toward reference librarians whenever suitable opportunities arise. Their goal is to get them accustomed to asking for help. Library planners discovered that these students find the library's silence and imposing architecture unnerving and may be reluctant to ask questions. In fact, they may waste precious time getting lost in the library's vast spaces. Finding opportunities for frequent interaction with the reference staff is very important. Because time is extremely limited, it's best for these students to know exactly where they're going each time they set out on a quest for library resources.

Customizing Information Services

You may remember that when library planners sought out these students, they were aided by the regularity of their schedules. Similarly, their academic programs have a sameness that the library can exploit as well. Nontraditional graduate students tend to be clustered in less than a dozen degree programs. Although each university's offerings are somewhat different, the larger master's programs tend to be in professional areas like education, counseling, and business administration. From the library's point of view, this greatly simplifies the job of meeting the students' needs. Since class scheduling is limited to one evening block and perhaps a few more class periods during the weekend, course offerings are necessarily limited. Master's students tend to take the same courses, with few opportunities for individual exploration. By working closely with the business administration faculty, it was possible for the reference staff in our fantasy library to get a good idea of the courses

Marian and her peers would be taking, as well as their probable research needs. This made it practical and even cost-effective to produce a series of instructional materials that seemed to be designed just for Marian.

A computer monitor near the information desk provides a continuous slide show introduction to the library, focusing on just the information that customers need to get started. Of course, it enthusiastically encourages customers to ask questions, both at the information and reference desks. Other service desks are highlighted as well. Note that I said that the computer monitor is near the information desk. Actually, it is in a pleasant little nook of its own surrounded by several lounge chairs. It is positioned precisely to attract the students who enter the library frazzled, cold, and windblown. It beckons them to sit down for a few minutes and get their bearings before charging ahead with their quest.

Attracting Attention

Most customers, whether undergrads or grad students, are attracted to moving images. The next time you go to a museum, take a good look at the places where visitors gather. Historical artifacts may actually get less attention than the media programs that accompany them. Video production requires considerable skill, but almost everyone can use presentation software to create an effective slide show. The real secret is correctly anticipating the needs of library customers. Armed with this understanding, as well as the basic requirements of the larger graduate programs, librarians can put together a remarkably effective library literacy program.

The public service staff in our fantasy library, both professional and paraprofessional, have received instruction in basic media literacy. They have access to the hardware and software needed to create simple media presentations. For example, there are several digital cameras at their disposal, and everyone has been trained in their basic functions. All staff computers are equipped with basic digital imaging software that allows them to enhance, crop, and otherwise customize the photographs they take. Among nontraditional graduate students, no need is greater than the need to use limited time as efficiently as possible. This means that pathfinders, media programs, and other instructional resources must be brief and strategically focused. A single page or a three-minute slide show might identify ABI/Inform, locate it on library computers, explain how it is useful, and provide simple search instructions. Of course, ABI is not the only important online resource in the field, but the student with a class in fifteen minutes cannot contemplate the full panoply of resources available to her. Nor is she interested in the complexities of advanced searching strategies.

Organizing Resources to Save the Customers' Time

How do these needs impact the way the library organizes its space and resources? To begin with, it is unwise to send an inexperienced student with only a few minutes to spare up to the fourth floor. In our fantasy library, only infrequently used print materials are stored in the remote reaches of the library building, and Marian is unlikely to need them. In fact, we can say with almost complete certainty that the printed materials Marian will need were published within the last ten years. In the case of professional journals, she will find almost all but recent issues in the library's online databases. Once again, our fantasy library has established policies that ensure that current periodicals and other heavily used materials are easy to find, shelved on or near the first floor. Scholarly materials that are used infrequently are kept on-site (our fantasy library would never make customers wait days for a book delivery), but they're in high-density storage. This means that warehousing space is kept to a minimum, and there's more room for people and the services they need.

The Personal Touch

Let's get back to Marian and her visit to our fantasy library. She is working on a class presentation and has come in search of some journal articles. She has already discovered that the library is a good place to get out of the rain, have a quick snack, and study for class in quiet comfort. She has also gotten some valuable tips on the parking situation from the friendly staff member at the information desk. This time, however, she will be doing some simple library research. Her new friend at the information desk, therefore, walks with her to the reference desk and introduces her to one of the reference librarians. Of course, the information staff are not always able to leave the desk, but they do so whenever possible. They know that it's a little difficult to see the reference desk, and they want to be sure their customers get off to a good start. They know that nontraditional students may be feeling intimidated by the large library, and it's best that they begin their quests under the watchful eye of the reference staff.

Establishing personal relationships with library staff is especially important for nontraditional students. They tend to believe that everyone on this vast, impersonal university campus knows what they're doing and where they're going; everyone, that is, but they themselves. Marian now knows two people to whom she can go for help. Other than her instructor and the other students in her class, these may be the only university staff members she knows by name. Marian would like to see these same people each time she visits the library, and a regular weekly staffing schedule encourages the development of these relationships. If this reference librarian works every Tuesday evening, Marian will be much more likely to seek out help than if a stranger is on the desk next week. Of course, it is not always possible to accommodate Marian's preference, but the librarian doing the scheduling should certainly make a good-faith effort.

When Only the Library Is Open

After a brief chat, the reference librarian points Marian to the ABI slide show or gives her the one-page pathfinder. Now she needs a library computer located close to the reference desk. No matter how well written the pathfinder, we must assume that customers who have rarely used a library computer or searched a periodical index will have questions. If they must cross the library to the information commons, they are unlikely to return to the reference desk with their questions. A group of computer workstations with half-hour time limits are positioned around the reference desk, and Marian is encouraged to come back if she has any problems. When Marian finds some useful articles, she will need to copy them, either on a computer disk or on paper. Library computers can accommodate flash memory devices, but, of course, Marian didn't know she would need one. Nor did she understand that a printing card or One Card was needed for paper copies. Marian has been merely wasting her time if she does all this work and then discovers she has no way to retain the articles she finds. Fortunately, the library has anticipated this possibility.

Even though evening/weekend programs are numerous, most university services operate only during regular business hours. Nontraditional students often find it difficult to purchase supplies, obtain student ID cards, see counselors, or even meet with their academic advisors. Since the library is one of the only campus facilities open both in the evening and on weekends, it can provide an invaluable service to students by anticipating at least some of the problems they encounter. Marian has less than an hour available to gather the materials she needs. She does not have time to leave the campus to purchase supplies, and she would never sacrifice her precious parking space to do so.

Because Marian spends very little time on campus and arrives directly from work, we can readily predict that she may come unprepared. The reference librarian had pointed out the One Card machine conveniently located beside the reference desk. Library planners made sure the machine could accept both coins and bills, but correct change may still be a problem for Marian. Libraries, in their desire to reduce theft, often refuse to handle cash. This can leave nontraditional students in a difficult position, unable to take advantage of lockers, use vending machines, or even feed the ravenous parking meter. Whether the library provides change machines, or designates a single secure service desk or an independent contractor like the café for this purpose, it should consider this an urgent need. Marian's library provides not only convenient printing card machines but other vending machines that dispense inexpensive flash drives, floppy disks and CDs, pencils, pens, and nonprescription pain relievers.

Equipping the 24-Hour Area

Although students taking evening classes find few university services available to them, those who must use the library's 24-hour study area are at an even greater disadvantage. Only the library is usually open at 2:00 a.m., and no one enjoys wandering around campus or around town in the wee hours searching for a cup of coffee. The 24-hour area in our fantasy library, therefore, has vending machines that dispense both fast food and essential supplies. Designated library staff members work closely with vending machine companies to assure that machines do not run out at night. Contracts with vendors spell out expected standards, and those that fail to maintain consistent quality (e.g., leave moldy sandwiches in their machines) are replaced.

ADVANCED STUDENTS WITH MULTIPLE NEEDS

The last of the students we will meet is Linda, a doctoral student in molecular biology. At the moment, Linda is working on her dissertation, and she is also showing signs of stress and fatigue. Linda knows that she must obtain her degree this year because she can't afford to remain jobless any longer. Of course, she worked as a teaching assistant on campus and found other pickup jobs to tide her over. However, her graduate work took longer than she anticipated, and now the pressure is really on. This semester, she has put everything aside and is spending long hours in the library.

Although it is helpful to be close to her research materials, the real reason she "lives" at the library is the discipline it imposes on her. She is trying to get away from temptation—the lure of a short nap, a long phone call, an even lengthier TV break. Even washing dishes can seem more appealing than the now-hated dissertation. Yes, hated! Students who are going through these last throes of graduate misery are sick and tired of research, writing, and especially their dissertation topics, which may have little to do with their interests. There are dozens of considerations that go into choosing a topic, such as their advisor's expertise and preferences, potential conflict with committee members, future employment, and feasible research designs. Over time, students' dissertations have become figurative albatrosses hung around their necks.

Their Own Personal Librarian

Each time Linda meets with her dissertation committee, she leaves with new assignments and added frustration. Has she looked into this? Why hasn't she included Professor Whosit's research? What is the basis for this statement? Surely she needs better documentation than that "two-bit hack." Linda's first stop after these exasperating meetings is usually her friend Henry. Henry is actually the assistant director for access services in our fantasy library. All librarians are assigned at least a small number of doctoral students, and Henry now has six. He is not a molecular biologist, but he does hold an undergraduate science degree, and he has a good knowledge of the way science literature is organized. Doctoral students are assigned a librarian when they first sign up for dissertation credits. If they would like to be assigned their own personal librarian earlier in their programs, their requests are always honored.

Henry's students are usually limited to some area of biology, so his task is not an onerous one. He needn't possess the skills of a science librarian, but he does have to stay alert to new directions and new research tools. When librarians are assigned new students, they usually set up monthly meetings with them. As time goes on, they progress from more general information (for example, a personalized library tour) to the specific resources needed for dissertations. At first Linda didn't know why she needed a librarian, but once she began spending time in the library, she found herself frequently stopping by Henry's office. When an important interlibrary loan request did not arrive, Henry introduced her to the interlibrary loan staff, and together they figured out what was holding up the request.

One day Linda arrived at Henry's door in a panic. A committee member had tossed out the name of a major authority in her field. She hadn't dared admit her ignorance, had bluffed her way through the meeting, and had spent the last three hours desperately trying to find out who this mover and shaker might be. No matter where she looked, she could find nothing—not even a passing reference. This was when Henry really earned his stripes. He had the not-so-brilliant idea that Linda might be misspelling the name. He introduced her to the OPAC's internal truncation feature, thereby discovering a small treasure trove of references. Gradually, Linda learned a number of Henry's little tricks for making more effective use of the library. We sometimes think that a student who is nearing the end of her graduate program already knows more about relevant resources than we do. Although this may be true, there are many "insider" searching conventions of which they may be totally unaware. For example, Linda did not know that it was once standard library practice to interfile last names beginning with "Mc" with "Mac" in catalogs and indices. Students growing up with computers must still use some older printed resources, and the old, non-intuitive filing rules can cause them to miss important information.

Different Needs, Different Solutions

One of the reasons I've included Linda in this chapter is to point out how different student needs can be. On the other hand, I think libraries have traditionally done a better job serving the Lindas of academe than the Justins or the Marians. When we have an opportunity to establish a personal relationship with a student—when we see students as individuals, not as part of a herd—we bend over backward to help them. Neither Justin nor Marian has enough experience in libraries to seek us out or effectively communicate their needs. Our opinion of them may, therefore, be formed as a result of group behavior. For example, we may view freshmen and sophomores as loud and uncouth. It takes only one unfortunate experience with a cantankerous evening student railing about a missing reserve article to convince us that nontraditional students are disasters. With no understanding of their individual needs, we conclude that they have no business pursuing academic degrees and it's not our job to babysit them.

As long as we imagine that one size fits all, that our services need not be customized to meet individual needs, we will never succeed in effectively serving our customers. Nor can we satisfy their needs if we decide that they should somehow be different from who they are. It is not our business to decide that Marian should have more time available, or that Justin should be able to concentrate on his work without caffeine and inviting library spaces. Success will continue to evade us until we accept our customers as full partners and embrace their ideas as we would those of library professionals.

RESOURCES

Bennett, Scott. *Libraries Designed for Learning.* Washington, DC: Council on Library and Information Resources, 2003, 4.

————. "Righting the Balance." In *Library as Place: Rethinking Roles, Rethinking Space.* Washington, DC: Council on Library and Information Resources, 2005, 12.

Council on Library and Information Resources. *Library as Place: Rethinking Roles, Rethinking Space.* CLIR Publication no. 129. Washington, DC: Council on Library and Information Resources, 2005. Available at www.clir.org/pubs/reports/pub129/pub129.pdf.

Demas, Sam. "From the Ashes of Alexandria: What's Happening in the College Library?" In *Library as Place: Rethinking Roles, Rethinking Space.* Washington, DC: Council on Library and Information Resources, 2005, 20–25.

Freeman, Geoffrey T. "The Library as Place: Changes in Learning Patterns, Collections, Technology, and Use." In *Library as Place: Rethinking Roles, Rethinking Space.* Washington, DC: Council on Library and Information Resources, 2005, 3.

Shill, Harold B., and Shawn Tonner. "Does the Building Still Matter? Usage Patterns in New, Expanded, and Renovated Libraries, 1995–2002." *College and Research Libraries* 65, no. 2 (March 2004): 123–50.

Starkweather, Wendy, and Kenneth Marks. "What If You Build It, and They Keep Coming and Coming and Coming?" *Library Hi Tech* 23, no. 1 (2005): 22–33.

See the book's website for additional materials to help you evaluate your library from the customer's point of view: www.ala.org/editions/extras/woodward09768.

5

TRANSFORMING SPACES ON TIGHT BUDGETS

Academic libraries of the past were often beautiful buildings, inspiring edifices that reflected the lofty place of books in the academic community. They mirrored the world of which they were an important part. While older libraries attracted users through their obvious importance and beauty, modern libraries offer a less exalting experience. Their vastness, especially those endless stack ranges, can dehumanize the library experience.

LIVING WITH OLDER LIBRARIES

Most of the 1950s, 1960s, and early 1970s were good years for academic libraries. The economy was doing well, and it seemed as if every college or university was obtaining a low-interest loan or government grant to build a new library. Unfortunately, this period of academic plenty corresponded with perhaps the ugliest era of modern architecture. Unadorned slabs of cement were typical of library design, as were huge spaces devoid of architectural features or other decoration. Architects of the period were rebelling against the ornate, cluttered look of older public buildings. Inspired by trendsetters like Mies van der Rohe and Frank Lloyd Wright, they designed structures with clean, unbroken lines, with nothing interrupting the flow of space. Unfortunately, the wear and tear that buildings experience as they age becomes even more obvious with such designs. Because there is nothing else to capture our attention, the eye is drawn to stains, tears, scratches, graffiti, and dirt in general.

Never again have funds for new libraries been so abundant. Many larger academic libraries are still housed in these same buildings. Because their simplicity makes them easy to add on to, planners often find it more cost-effective to expand them than start from scratch. However, even with remodeling and new additions, these buildings are not comfortable places for people to work and congregate in. All across the country, libraries are on waiting lists. They're waiting to advance, one notch at a time, toward the magic moment when they will be approved for an all-new building. The problem is that academic campuses are intensely political places and the library is essentially apolitical, serving the needs of all members of the academic community. Library capital projects may be deferred again and again as budgets plummet and competing departments vie for power.

Although most academic libraries share similar problems, it is the larger university libraries that may suffer most. Projects that might be manageable in a smaller library, like replacing worn carpeting, cost hundreds of thousands of dollars in these gigantic edifices. For this reason, decades pass during which budget requests for remodeling and renovations are repeatedly refused. Librarians experience a sense of helplessness, and the vastness of their building prevents them from feeling any sense of responsibility or ownership. It's not their fault that their building is ugly and uninviting. If the university wants an attractive library, then the university will have to pay for it.

Large, Cold Libraries

Students, however, are not interested in who is at fault. All they know is that they are uncomfortable in the library. They prefer study spaces that are on a more human scale. Jason is a student who is presently coping with just such a library. His advisor suggested that he begin spending an hour or two a day in his university library, and, of course, he was always vaguely aware of the library's presence. It occupies a central position and is one of the largest, most imposing buildings on campus. Uniform university signage has brought Jason to the main entrance, and we find him entering the library through one of the large glass doors.

Unlike the library described in the first chapter, the lobby has plenty of seating. In fact, that's about all it has. Jason can see thirty or more tired, uncomfortable, 1970s-era sofas lined up in rows, marching down the length of the cavernous space. Stone panels on the walls and stone tiles on the floor are certainly intended to last, but their grayish color is anything but inviting. The boxy sofas in hard-wearing neutral tones do nothing to warm up the atmosphere. At first glance, Jason sees nothing but sofas. Surely there must be more to the library than this. No library directory is in evidence, nor are there directional signs that might lead him into the library proper. Taking a second look, he discovers several doors with cryptic signs like "North Tower" and "South Tower." It appears that he must go through one of these doors, but there is no indication of what lies beyond each. In front of one, he sees a sign mounted on an easel. Perhaps this will provide some information, but no. When he gets close enough to read it, the sign merely admonishes him to turn off his cell phone and refrain from eating in the library.

Large Libraries Equal Confused Customers

Large academic libraries are extremely confusing. If two or more additions have been attached to the original structure over the course of time, they become labyrinths practically requiring GPS systems to find one's way. Even experienced graduate students have difficulty finding their way around, so we can expect undergraduates to need a lot of help. When students enter the library, they need guidance immediately. Large university libraries are truly vast, and students may literally walk for miles. They need to be intercepted when they first arrive, but they are easily overwhelmed. Information must be presented in a way that is appropriate to their immediate needs. Jason has no idea what lies beyond the lobby, and because he has rarely used any type of library, he is unfamiliar with the kinds of spaces and services that libraries typically provide.

In addition, he's feeling uncomfortable and overwhelmed. The vast spaces and stone-hard surfaces are intimidating, nothing like the places where he usually spends his time. If the library building's alterations and renovations include links to other campus buildings, foot traffic may be especially heavy. It may be difficult to pause and get one's bearings amid the sea of students hurrying to their 10:00 classes. Remember that as a race, we have spent very little of our collective existence in large interior spaces. We humans, who once lived in caves, feel comfortable in small, cozy nooks, and it requires considerable work on the part of architects and librarians to make a vast academic library feel welcoming.

Let's back up to the moment when Jason entered the library. The space in which he found himself was actually designed as a way of connecting the original library building with a large addition. It was the creation not of the library staff but of the architects who found it useful both for integrating the two buildings and for providing a visually impressive main entrance. From the library staff's point of view, the lobby is just there. All their activities are housed in one wing or the other. The lobby is "no-man's-land."

The Welcome Center

It's fortunate that we are beginning our tour with the lobby because it's so fixable. A few thousand dollars can make a profound difference here. Because the lobby has little in the way of a defined library function, we are free to make it what we want it to be—and what we want is a sort of welcome center. Our task is to create a small environment that makes Jason feel comfortable and confident that he will have a positive library experience. It must also be a space that offers enough information so he can achieve his first goal, information that is presented in a form that he can easily assimilate. At the same time, a large number of people may be coming and going. Their needs may be completely different from Jason's.

Let's begin with the atmosphere. You'll recall that there is almost no color in the lobby. Walls and floor tiles are a pale beige/tan/gray stone. Sofas are neutral in color, with stainless steel accents. Although restaurants emphasize color, homes have color schemes, and even supermarkets are color coordinated, large libraries are often afraid of color. Perhaps librarians were forced to live with once-trendy colors like harvest gold for too many years and swore they would never again select strong colors. It's certainly true that today's terribly trendy colors will be despised tomorrow. More likely, however, when they were confronted with paint, carpet, and upholstery samples, it was just easier for library administrators to choose neutral shades that would not clash with one another. Even professional designers sometimes avoid color because it is so often a point of disagreement. If you've ever served on a committee that decided such matters, you'll remember the intense reactions some people have to certain colors. In abandoning color, however, we make a major mistake. Color has a tremendous impact on our moods and the way we feel about spaces. Even the absence of color affects us strongly.

Meeting Customer Needs

Getting back to Jason as he is entering the library, we must ask ourselves what his needs are at this moment. Because he hasn't come for a specific journal article or other item from the collection, he very likely has at least two important needs. The first is to be reassured and encouraged. He wants to be a more conscientious student, and he needs reassurance that the library can help him achieve his goal. His first impressions of the library should confirm that this is a pleasant, comfortable place in which he can productively spend his time. It is a place where he can study, free of most of the distractions of his dormitory. It is a place where he will not be viewed as an intruder but as a welcome customer, encouraged to take advantage of the library's many services.

At the same time, Jason needs to be informed. Even though his goal is a modest one and does not require knowledge of the library's cataloging system or sophisticated skills, he needs to know where to go next. Which doorway will bring him to a pleasant study area, and which leads to a stairwell or broom closet? Other students may need more specific information about library services, but they will not be able to absorb elaborate directions. The space that confronts visitors as they enter the library should be designed specifically and deliberately to meet such needs.

Librarians have amassed a wealth of experience dealing with students, and so it is not difficult for them to predict these needs. Students arriving directly from class often need restrooms and someplace to unwind for a few minutes before they tackle an assignment. Like Marian in the last chapter, students are often tired, since they may be juggling a job, a full schedule of courses, and an active social life. If they must spend twenty minutes or more in search of a book or tape, their weariness will give way to hostility, and in the future they will find many ways to avoid the library. Students may even be having difficulty staying awake, so a cup of coffee may be high on their list of urgent needs.

Helping Customers Feel Oriented

How can the lobby area make it clear that the library is eager to welcome customers and meet their needs? How can this first, brief experience leave a positive and lasting impression? Let's begin with color, since that is usually the first thing we notice about a space. One library I recently visited erected a free-standing (but very stable) accent wall that faced visitors as they came in the main entrance. It was far enough away from the doorway that it did not obstruct traffic, but it was so brightly colored that it immediately attracted attention. Occupying much of the wall was a very large but highly simplified library floor plan. Unlike most commercially designed building directories, it was intended only to get customers headed in the right direction. More precise information would come later. Like the wall, it was painted in bright colors intended to attract attention. Designed by a library staff member and painted by a talented student assistant, the sign was actually made of some large sheets of masonite on which were shown similarly large rectangles of color representing the different library areas. The floor plan included only very general information that could be easily absorbed in a single glance. Limiting content to very basic information also meant that the floor plan needn't be changed very often. Nevertheless, libraries have a habit of changing the location of both resources and services for a variety of reasons. When this happens, the floor plan must be updated or it can cause a great deal of frustration.

Because students may forget even the very limited dose of information presented on the sign, why not place a literature rack beside it and provide printed copies of the floor plan? Such a rack, however, should be filled only with the kind of general information that students will immediately find useful. It should not be filled with pizza coupons or library pathfinders that you're trying to use up. Because the library's mission is to inform its customers, helpful guides produced by the university should be available but not here, not when customers are entering the library. Our goal is to help them focus on their own information needs and on their reasons for coming to the library. By reducing information clutter, we can make it easier for them to take that next step.

WHERE HELP IS NEEDED

Although I am jumping ahead with my story, I can't resist reminding you of the sign described earlier. You may remember that it sat on an easel in front of a set of double doors and admonished visitors to turn off their cell phones. The easel was set up in such a way that library users exiting from the room beyond the double doors, preparatory to leaving the library, were confronted with the back of the sign. It read "Have a question? You can ask anyone on the library staff." This is, of course, very important information. It might have made a confused student more willing to ask that staff member staring intently at her computer screen for help. However, neither he nor the other students will see this sign until they are leaving the library.

This brings up an important subject. Would it be a good idea to locate an information desk in the lobby? Although university libraries usually have several service desks, they can usually afford to staff only one information desk (actually, to be perfectly truthful, many university libraries don't even bother to provide one, but that is another matter). Is the lobby the best place to locate the information desk? The answer will be different depending on the nature of the space. For example, is there too much noise and hubbub in the lobby to communicate clearly? Is the lobby so cut off from the rest of the library that directions will be unnecessarily complicated? It may be better to rely on a directory to get customers into the library proper. Ideally, the information desk should be located where the largest number of library users find themselves confused and don't know where they're going. Just as they are discovering that they are in a very large and confusing space, they also discover the information desk, where a staff member can help them deal with the confusion. If the lobby is a more integral part of the library, then it may indeed be the best place to locate an information desk.

Other Appetizing Features

A short expanse of brightly colored wall can help erase the sense of a vast, cavernous space. Another free-standing wall might be positioned elsewhere in the lobby to reduce the apparent dimensions of the space to a more human scale if it does not interfere with traffic. Such walls might provide an opportunity for a mini art gallery, another opportunity to introduce color and make the space more interesting. Because lobby areas are usually tiled and easy to clean, they can become excellent locations for a café. Cafés provide a wonderful opportunity to introduce more color and make the library appear more inviting. The enticing aroma of coffee and baked goods (think cinnamon rolls) further raises expectations. Because cafés attract students, they make the library appear to be an active, popular place. Efficient, self-contained coffee carts can be located almost anyplace without expensive renovations.

Lockers are, of course, important to students, but a lobby lined with lockers is uninviting, to say the least. If at all possible, locate lockers and other unattractive but necessary functions off the lobby area. Then consider how the remaining lobby space can be redesigned to be more inviting. Use color in places where it can be easily changed a few years from now, when today's hues are outdated. New, trendier shades will make the lobby appear more up-to-date. If you don't have the kind of walls that will withstand a nuclear blast, it's usually relatively easy to repaint them and recover a few accent sofas and lounge chairs at relatively low cost. Avoid using a bright color where it is likely to remain for years to come, making the library look dated and unfashionable. Good-quality tables and study carrels have long life expectancies and may remain in the library for as long as fifty years. Those mauve accent stripes and teal surfaces we've been seeing will soon be looking very dated.

Seating Preferences

Even in the lobby area, comfortable seating is important. Customers will probably not be sitting here very long, but a comfortable chair is something they will notice. Some students will want to sit together, while others will prefer to sit alone. Most of us feel uncomfortable if we must look directly at a stranger occupying the seat across from us. Don't arrange seating as if the chairs and sofas were soldiers marching in military precision. You'd be uncomfortable with this arrangement in your own home, and there's no reason why students using the library would find it any more accept-able. Like your home, the lobby will look more inviting with the addition of paintings, green plants, and other attractive decorations (the plants needn't be real, but they shouldn't be covered with a thick layer of dust). However, unlike your home, a few large features will be more effective and easier to maintain than a plethora of small ones. If no staff members are stationed in the lobby, it is important that these decorative additions be permanently installed and yet easily replaceable. I recall one librarian complaining that she made the library nice and then students trashed it. She seemed to blame the entire student body for this heinous crime. Vandalism is a reality and must be considered, but most students are not vandals. They appreciate nice things and treat them respectfully. It is not impossible to create an attractive environment that can withstand abuse.

THE USE AND MISUSE OF SIGNAGE

Because our library tour is an imaginary one, we can make these changes in the wink of an eye and present Jason with a positive first impression. We can also provide some very basic information, which he can take with him as he explores the library. Jason has now crossed the lobby and is passing through the double doorway into the central part of the library. Now what? While the floor plan consisted mainly of colorful shapes, the real library is highly complex, housing many stack areas, study spaces, service desks, computer labs, and obscurely titled doors. Restrooms may be tucked away in remote spots that require a GPS navigator to reach them. What's missing in most large academic libraries is a coherent, carefully thought-out signage system. My own informal survey of large academic libraries indicates that their sig-nage is less helpful than the signs in their smaller cousins. In fact, it may be almost nonexistent. Library staff members mark or identify the materials in their own departments, but no one seems to be responsible for the very large, general signs that are needed to guide library customers through the vast, uncharted spaces.

Let's take the map area as an example. Cabinets containing maps are probably labeled, as are the individual drawers of the cabinets. Tent signs or Lucite-framed copy paper may indicate general categories like geographical regions or topographical maps. Most materials are organized in a logical ar-rangement that is more or less explained in other signs, notices, and finding aids. In other words, once customers find the right area, they fall under the "protection" of the map department and are able to take advantage of the librarians' expert ability to organize information.

Jason, of course, isn't looking for maps, but there's a very nice, quiet study area on the third floor that is exactly what he needs. Perhaps Jason noticed the study area on the floor plan, but how can he get to it? Both stairwells and elevators are hidden from view, and no signs point visitors toward them. In fact, the 300 feet between Jason and the elevators might be seen as a kind of maze of new book displays, study carrels, literature racks, and miscellaneous media storage units. Without clear signage that he can follow from the entrance to the elevators, he will waste a lot of time and energy. Even if signs are provided, Jason may not notice them. They may be bolted to convenient columns rather than positioned where incoming customers will actually see them. The type font may be too small to read from a distance, or the terminology used may mean nothing to the general public. In fact, the colors chosen for text and background may look the same to color-blind visitors (who are surprisingly numerous).

Signage Is an Ongoing Responsibility

As I mentioned, signage in large academic libraries tends to be less effective than in any other type of library. Of course, that's partly because of their size and the long distances customers must travel to reach their destinations. However, staff members in large university libraries also tend to feel little sense of ownership of their buildings. In the complex library hierarchy, the library building is always someone else's responsibility. Perhaps a professional signage system was part of the capital outlay budget when the library was built. From the very beginning, those signs may have had limited usefulness because it's very difficult to predict traffic patterns and user habits before a library is fully operational. Collections planned for one area end up being moved to another. Service desks are relocated to get them out from behind a column or to get a better view of arriving customers. As time passes, administrators are reluctant to change signs because it would mean a large and costly project. Existing signs may gradually become invisible to the library staff.

In a small library, staff might simply get out their foam board, ink-jet printers, and spray adhesive to create a raft of new signs. This do-it-yourself way of thinking is not common in large academic libraries, however. Instead, we tend to find a lot of tattered paper signs with no thought to organization, or perhaps no signs at all. One very innovative academic library I visited requested funds for a renovation project that included extensive new signage. A number of interested library staff members were brought together to identify the signs that were most needed, the places where customers were most likely to need assistance, and the ways in which the signs could be integrated with one another to be most effective. The project generated so much enthusiasm that staff members wanted to implement their plan immediately. However, their renovation request was turned down, and the signage project was about to be deep-sixed.

It was then that the group decided that the project was too important to delay. They would test the system they had designed with temporary signs created, like those in smaller libraries, with foam board and ink-jet printers. Because a lot of work had been expended on the project, the resulting signs looked surprisingly professional. As it turned out, the renovation project was delayed for six years. During that period, library customers were able to find their way around the library thanks to a well-designed signage system. When funds were finally available for costly professional signage, the library staff had already tested each sign and each location, making changes where appropriate.

Signage 101

A great deal of study has been devoted to signs and the way customers interact with them. Some signs capture our attention while others do not. Providing precisely the right amount of information at the right moment can totally transform the customer's experience. Librarians tend to complain that their customers never read signs, so why should they bother? This attitude implies that it is the customer's fault for failing to read the minds of the library staff. Hardly any other profession understands the importance of meeting information needs like librarians. We understand the difficulties our customers face when performing Boolean searches, but we fail to understand the problems they encounter when trying to find their way through our libraries.

Signs must be presented at decision points, at those moments when customers pause and look around, wondering whether to turn right or left. Signs must be visible, not hidden behind columns or stacks, and they must call attention to themselves. If an orange sign with black letters tells Jason to turn left, his eyes will be more likely to hone in on the next orange sign with black letters. He may not notice that green sign with a different type font. Of course, while Jason is finding his way to the elevator, other customers will be leaving the elevators or have other needs requiring signs to direct them. Again, a lot of thought has been put into the ways in which signage can meet a wide variety of customer needs without becoming confusing. In fact, large university libraries usually have a number of books on signage in their collections. It is not necessary to create a jungle of signs, but it is necessary to create a unified, coherent signage system.

Multiple Points of Entry

Once again, we wave our magic wand and Jason is able to make his way to the elevators without difficulty. However, by now the floor plan he viewed in the lobby is a dim memory. Was that study area on the second or the third floor? The only signs visible near the elevators tell the user that these are elevators 1, 2, 3, and 4. It happens that two of the elevators don't go to the top floor and only one stops at the mezzanine, but the copy paper sign containing this information has long since disappeared. Jason decides that he will get off on the second floor and see if the quiet study area is there.

Unfortunately, the elevator opens into a stack area with nothing to indicate what lies beyond. In reality, this is an entrance, the entrance to the second floor. An elevator plunges the library customer into a new space in a disorienting way. It's easy to get oneself mentally turned around. Just as Jason was most confused when he first entered the lobby, he is also likely to need direction when he first arrives on a new floor. It's a sudden, disorienting experience, and some guidance is almost always needed.

To be effective, signage must focus on the customer's need for information at precisely the moment when that information is most needed. When Jason approached the elevator on the main floor, he needed to know enough about the areas and services located on the other floors to get off at the right level. At that moment, he was focused on finding the right elevator, entering the elevator without tripping, pressing the right button, and arriving at the desired floor. However, when he emerges from the elevator, he has a different information need. He finds himself in a large, confusing space and needs immediate guidance. That information must be directly in front of Jason or he will not see it. For example, a sign suspended from the ceiling might provide this information, or it might be outside Jason's field of vision as he emerges from the elevator. A floor-mounted sign might be a better choice, but it must be facing Jason as he leaves the elevator. A sign affixed to the elevator wall will be visible to customers entering the elevator but not to Jason.

Jason's needs are not unlike those of thousands of other students. If we continue to encourage him by making his visits to the library pleasant and successful, he will explore our other services. In fact, it is not difficult to predict and prepare for the library usage patterns that are typical of undergraduates. Jason is a customer, as are all the students who attend our university. They can choose to avail themselves of our services or they can ignore them. Graduate students' needs are more complicated, but again, we have worked with hundreds, perhaps even thousands of grad students and we understand how they approach the library. Good customer service is just as essential to the success and continued well-being of the library as it is to any commercial establishment. Not only our signage but the library's actual organization must reflect those usage patterns. When we make decisions about space needs and services, it is those needs, not our own convenience, that must tip the scales.

LIGHTING LARGE BUILDINGS

Thanks to our magic wand, Jason has now found the quiet study area, and he's all set to spend an hour or two preparing for his next test. He need not fear that his roommate will blast the stereo or his friends will entice him into hanging out with them. No TV or DVD player tempts him, and the library furniture will effectively discourage him from napping. However, as he begins to read, he realizes that it's hard to see the text. There's no problem with his eyesight; the cause of the trouble is the dim lighting. Looking up, he sees that lighting fixtures, each intended to hold four 4-foot fluorescent tubes, have been installed the length and breadth of the ceiling. Looking closer, Jason realizes that the number of tubes in each fixture has been reduced to two. In other words, only half the fluorescent lamps intended to light the room are in use, so the room is only half as bright as originally intended. Actually, even less light is available because a number of the fluorescent tubes have burned out.

In universities across the country, administrators have made the decision to reduce energy use by drastically cutting back on the light in their academic libraries. The situation Jason encounters—a shadowy library where customer eyestrain goes unnoticed—is common. Windows are often completely absent in these areas, so it may be impossible to read for any length of time without experiencing a headache. Flashlights may even be needed to read call numbers in the stacks. In addition to making such areas unsuitable for study, poor lighting makes a space look gray and dingy. Not only do they look depressing, but such spaces with their deep shadows can even be dangerous.

Measuring Light Levels

Before the lighting in Jason's library can be improved, the staff must fully understand the extent of the problem. Librarians charged with building responsibilities need access to a light meter, a relatively inexpensive device used to measure the exact amount of light falling on a spot. The measure of light levels most often used by architects and lighting contractors is the foot-candle. At table or study carrel height, 50 to 55 foot-candles provide the best reading light. It is often impossible to achieve this level throughout the entire study area, but nowhere should the level fall below about 25 to 30 foot-candles. Getting used to a light meter takes some time (the numbers change at dizzying speed), but with a little practice, staff can quickly determine which areas of the library are most deficient in lighting. Armed with this information, the next challenge is to improve light conditions without waiting for a major renovation project.

Energy conservation is indeed a concern for all universities, but a lighting policy like the one described above places far too much of the burden on library customers and seriously interferes with the library's ability to meet their needs. In no other campus building is light more important to a successful program than in the library. Other, much less draconian measures will yield savings but will not cause customers to flee the library.

Full-Spectrum Lighting

Universities often purchase the cheapest fluorescent tubes they can find, installing them throughout the campus regardless of actual lighting needs. These low-quality lamps, which can be purchased in bulk for as little as fifty cents each, give off light in a narrow range of the spectrum and burn out much more quickly than higher-quality lamps. If librarians put a little effort into investigating the choices available, they would discover that full-spectrum lamps provide far better lighting and ultimately cost little more than their bargain-basement competitors. Armed with accurate information about precisely how much light is needed in each area and how much is supplied by each lamp, the library can develop a plan that neither squanders energy recklessly nor leaves library customers in the dark. Although these high-quality tubes initially cost several times as much, they also last several times as long. This means that the university's maintenance department saves on labor costs, while superior lighting and energy savings are also achieved.

It is not necessary to wait until funds become available for a major library renovation project to tackle the lighting situation. The same fixtures accommodate both high- and low-quality fluorescent tubes. In fact, it may be possible to achieve better lighting throughout the library with little or no increase in overall costs. However, that does not mean it will be easy to accomplish the needed changes. The political or bureaucratic environment that characterizes most universities can pose a nearly insurmountable hurdle. The support of your university's maintenance department is essential, so establishing a good relationship with the department head is a number one priority. It may be necessary, however, to enlist the support of a high-level university administrator to authorize the needed change in purchasing procedures. Some library directors have been successful in re-lamping one floor or one large area as an experiment. The results are often so dramatic that it becomes much easier to convince decision makers of the need for change.

A SAFE, WELCOMING PLACE

Since we've spent quite a bit of time with Jason, perhaps we should turn our attention to a graduate student. Crystal is a doctoral student working on a literature review. There was a time when most of the materials she needed were physically located in the library or were available through the library's interlibrary loan department. However, since her review will be composed primarily of journal articles, she can now locate most of her materials online. What Crystal really needs is a place where she is forced to focus on her work, where there are no tempting distractions and she has little choice but to get down to business. Crystal, therefore, seeks out a remote area of the library where she won't have to listen to undergraduates discussing their love life.

Such areas are sometimes ominously silent. Seating areas and stack ranges seem to go on and on to infinity, but no other students are seated at the study carrels or browsing through the stacks. Crystal makes herself comfortable at one of the tables and begins unloading her backpack. Suddenly, out of the silence, she hears a noise. She listens, but the room is once again silent. Even though Crystal is not an impressionable young woman, she can't help but feel anxious. Terrible tragedies like the Virginia Tech shootings are not far from the thoughts of many students, and safety is an important concern.

Most university libraries are experiencing a drop in usage, and those far-distant stack areas were never hubs of activity. Libraries have a responsibility to provide not only actual security for their students but also the feeling of being in a safe, welcoming place. An experience similar to Crystal's occurred to me just a few months ago. I was visiting a large university library and required some rarely circulated materials. These were shelved in just such a deserted area. When some unexplained sounds made me feel uncomfortable, I quickly found the materials I needed, gathered up my notes, and prepared to relocate to a more populated part of the library. As I was leaving, however, I noticed a door with a small window. Peeking through it, I discovered a work area with at least four library staff members toiling at desks and tables.

Had Crystal or I known that there were library staff members working nearby, we would have felt much more comfortable. Yet it often seems as if staff members are hiding from library customers. Imagine bringing those staff members out into the public area. We tend to assume that we still need the same large backroom work areas that libraries required fifty years ago. And yet computers have greatly reduced the amount of space needed to perform many library tasks, as well as the clutter that once accompanied them.

Perhaps your library houses its government documents staff in a work area that is invisible to library customers. Consider what would be involved in making them more visible. If staff members are working in a remote area of the library, they obviously won't be besieged by questions that interrupt their work. However, their presence may make all the difference in assuring nervous students that the library is a safe and hospitable place in which to spend their time. Although it's relatively infrequent, crime does occur in university libraries. Purses are snatched and backpacks are stolen. Library staff members represent authority, and their presence can deter many criminals, especially prowling juvenile delinquents, from setting up shop in the library.

Nevertheless, the decision to move staff members into public areas brings with it a number of challenges. For example, staff must make a certain amount of noise as they go about their duties, so peaceful coexistence in a quiet study area might be difficult. On the other hand, the presence of the library staff might discourage noisy students from disrupting others. The real hurdle might be the library culture itself. In chapter 3, we discussed the reluctance of some public service staff members to spend time in public areas. Although we've put a great deal of effort into hiring staff who enjoy being around other people, there's plenty of evidence that some library employees still seek "hidey-holes" away from the public. Sometimes we're not even aware of their discomfort until they give one flawed reason after another for remaining in their sanctuaries. As academic library staffs continue to shrink and the emphasis moves away from collection and toward services, these staff members become a liability. Although we want all staff members to enjoy their jobs and feel comfortable with their surroundings, the library must be able to achieve its goals.

PERSONALIZING LARGE SPACES

Even in this remote corner of the library, Crystal wants to be able to use her laptop computer. That requires connectivity and an electrical outlet. Wireless access throughout the building is usually feasible, even in a large library, but a major rewiring project is costly. Every planned improvement is more expensive in a large library. Projects that might be completed with end-of-year budget savings in a smaller institution become mammoth in mega-libraries. However, there is really no need to include the entire building in every proposed improvement. Changes needn't be made on a grand scale. Small improvements regularly incorporated into the library budget can often be more effective than large ones. In fact, they provide more opportunities to experiment, and mistakes are less costly.

However, the response you'll often hear from administrators is "Why bother?" or "Why waste money? All that wiring will be redone during the renovation." If we are really faithful to our customers, there is only one answer. We can't sit back and continue to discourage customers from using the library when productive steps could be taken. Besides, small experiments can serve as educational experiences, providing the staff with a clearer understanding of the needs of customers. In other words, you can improve the lighting in one wing and then see whether customers seek out that space. Purchasing carpeting for such a vast acreage is truly mind-boggling, but replacing the worn carpet by the second-floor elevator is doable, especially if the library held on to the excess carpet the last time it was replaced and did not allow it to be carried out with the carpet installers. You can add electrical outlets to an infrequently used area, advertise the improvements, and then watch what happens.

Note that I mention advertising here because I consider it absolutely essential. Customers may be less likely to discover attractive features and services in a large library because they never happen to come upon them. Although most academic libraries fail to market their services as effectively as they might, they are even less inclined to advertise individual library spaces. Customers may have no idea of the extent of the library, possibly assuming it ends at the first floor. They may be completely unaware of smaller, more personally appealing spaces hidden among the endless stack ranges. "Think small" is actually a pretty good motto for university librarians when it comes to meeting customer needs. Individuals need small spaces that are designed to meet small, personal needs. As librarians and fellow human beings, we understand these needs. We needn't catch that nasty old institutional monument disease.

RESOURCES

Bennett, S. "First Questions for Designing Higher Education Learning Spaces." *Journal of Academic Librarianship* 33, no. 1 (January 2007): 14–26.

Foote, S. M. "Changes in Library Design: An Architect's Perspective." *portal: Libraries and the Academy* 4, no. 1 (January 2004): 41–59, esp. 42.

Gibson, C., et al. "The Johnson Center Library at George Mason University." *Reference Services Review* 35, no. 2 (2007): 322–30.

Jones, W. G. "Library Buildings at the Threshold of Change." In *Advances in Librarianship* 30 (2006): 201–32.

"Saltire: A Learning Building—A Building to Learn From." *Multimedia Information and Technology* 33, no. 2 (May 2007): 62–64.

Seaman, S. "The Library as Learning Environment: Space Planning in an Academic Library." *Colorado Libraries* 32, no. 1 (Winter 2006): 5–7.

Shill, H. B., and S. Tonner. "Does the Building Still Matter? Usage Patterns in New, Expanded, and Renovated Libraries, 1995–2002." *College and Research Libraries* 65, no. 2 (March 2004): 123–50.

Weaver, M. "Flexible Design for New Ways of Learning." *Library and Information Update* 5, no. 7/8 (July/August 2006): 54–55.

6

MAKING THE TRANSITION TO A TWENTY-FIRST-CENTURY LIBRARY

Libraries, essentially identical to those of the 1970s except in decor and technology, are being designed by architects at this very moment. When confronted by administrators who mistakenly announce that the book is dead, by faculty who demand that their deathless prose be enshrined in printed and bound journals, and by architects who are focused on design awards, librarians may feel helpless. However, although the future is shrouded in haze, we have a much clearer picture of the library's role in tomorrow's academic world than do architects, administrators, or other members of the academic community. We have an obligation to both our profession and our libraries to act on our vision.

The twentieth-century library was built to accommodate printed resources. As we plan for the twenty-first century, we are reasonably certain that libraries will continue to purchase print, but survival depends on expanding services far beyond those of the traditional academic library. Perhaps the best way to approach the twenty-first century is to focus on the total student experience and the ways in which the library can enhance it. This chapter is intended to awaken your imaginations by presenting a welter of ideas that other librarians have tried and found to be effective. In one sense, they're all good ideas because they have all had a positive impact on some academic libraries, but they're not all for you. Some require a major investment in staff or expensive building modifications; others cost almost nothing. The majority fall somewhere in the middle.

STRATEGIES FOR THE TWENTY-FIRST CENTURY

This list of innovations is really intended to help you see your own library in a new way. As you consider whether this or that change might work in your environment, you may discover that there are some even better ideas that have been percolating in the back of your mind. You know which academic departments are willing to work collaboratively with the library and which are more reticent. You know which programs are growing and which may be fading out of existence. This kind of insider information is essential when you consider possible changes. Naturally, you want to get the most "bang for the buck" by impacting the largest number of library users. Thus some of these suggestions may seem like a lot of work expended for doubtful results.

You'll notice that the list is not limited to what we usually consider the public service departments of the library. Rather, all of the suggestions are intended to enhance the public's experience of the library. All are intended to meet the needs of some segment of the library's customer base. As you consider each strategy, think about who would be affected by the change or service. Would faculty members use the library more? Would they be more likely to incorporate the library into their teaching? Would a service encourage students to "hang out" in the library? Would a change enhance the image of the library in the minds of administrators? If you can't imagine some group of customers for whom this service would make a significant difference, then your efforts can be better spent on something else.

The majority of these innovative ideas might be placed under the heading of "individualizing the library experience." Unlike academic libraries of the past, today's most successful libraries provide a variety of different types of facilities, services, and resources to meet the needs of a diverse customer base. This means that your customers should have considerable input in deciding which ideas should be implemented. When a new innovation "bombs," the reason often goes back to two basic mistakes. Customers were not closely involved in planning, and those targeted were not made aware that the library had something new and useful to offer them.

THE LIBRARY BUILDING

Let's begin with changes made to the library building itself, whether they merely involve moving some furniture around, purchasing some new equipment, remodeling, or major construction. Most projects can be scaled up or down depending on the size of your library. Try to keep yourself from automatically rejecting an idea because you don't have the money. Perhaps you don't have it now, but such an idea might be the seed around which an expansion plan might grow. Is there a way that you could achieve a similar result by redirecting some of your existing resources? At any rate, here are some creative possibilities you might consider.

Information Commons

The information commons concept has probably been a "hot topic" at many of the conferences you've attended during the past few years. Sometimes called the learning or knowledge commons, it can be broadly defined as a library space characterized by the availability of sophisticated information resources, shared by the academic community in an open-access environment. The term *commons* traditionally referred to the land or common ground that was once shared for grazing purposes. It's hard to imagine a library that wouldn't find this concept useful. Nearly every academic library has discovered that when you provide public computer workstations, you attract more students.

Although most of the library may be almost empty, the information commons tends to be a hub of activity. You might want to begin with the assumption that many customers, no matter what their specific needs might be, would like to have access to a computer. The name *information commons* does not necessarily refer to a single, confined space like the computer labs of the past. Are there ways that the far reaches of the library can be part of the commons? Wireless access, a roving technician, and power outlets to accommodate personal laptops would be a good start. Perhaps you want to keep your most sophisticated equipment under the library staff's watchful eye, but slightly older equipment fitted out with more security features might be made available in other areas, including the 24-hour facility. All commons are not created equal. They differ widely in their intended use and in their design and technical sophistication, as well as their size and location. Because the concept of the learning commons has swept the academic library world, the next chapter will be devoted to a more in-depth look at it than can be accommodated in this section.

Cafés, Coffee Shops, and Coffee Kiosks

Coffee shops are another very popular development in academic libraries. The impetus probably originated with the mega-bookstore chains that attract large numbers of customers with their comfortable ambience and trendy cafés. Librarians are readers, and we know how pleasant it is to curl up with a good book and a snack. Food, however, has traditionally been considered taboo in libraries, largely because of preservation concerns. However, most modern academic libraries do not retain printed materials as long as they once did. Information now becomes out-of-date with lightning speed, and networks like those of OCLC (Online Computer Library Center) and the Association of Research Libraries (ARL) have made it much more cost-effective to borrow infrequently used materials than to house them locally. Computers and media programs don't improve with coffee spills, but preservation is not really an issue with them.

Customers love library cafés, and there's growing evidence that cafés can play an important role in increasing library use. If poorly planned, however, food can create major custodial problems and damage valuable library resources. The decision to bring a café into the library is a very complicated one. If you are thinking about a café, one of the first questions you will probably want to answer is how you can make library collections coexist peacefully with food service. If a sizable proportion of your library's collection consists of rare books and manuscripts, they will need to be widely separated from sticky pastries. If such collections can be found throughout the library, then it may be impossible to completely segregate areas where food is permitted from areas where it is forbidden. Most academic libraries, however, can accommodate a café without a great deal of inconvenience.

Where would you locate a café? Is there a space that is not currently being fully used? Ideally, the area chosen should be as far from the book collection as possible. It should be large enough to include a preparation area and a space for tables and chairs. Modern, self-contained coffee carts house almost all the needed equipment and supplies but still require access to water and power. Remember that it's best for your customers to remain in the café and drink their lattes before they begin interacting with the library's collections. This means that the space needs to be large enough to accommodate your potential customers. Nevertheless, it is unrealistic to think that food and drink will not find their way to other parts of the library. Because food service is tightly regulated by local governments, you will also want to find out about local regulations and identify the government agency that inspects food service establishments.

Your café will be more successful if its hours of operation do not depend on the library's hours. Most cafés are built around coffee, and coffee is drunk mainly in the morning. Ideally, you will want to open at 7:00 a.m. A separate entrance can be useful in this regard, but it's not really necessary. Since it's a good idea to keep food in a separate area, it is helpful to have natural barriers between food and books. A separate floor, wing, or room is preferable, but simple solutions like wrought iron railings will work too. Many libraries find basements to be a good place to put a café if the wiring is up to code and fire safety does not pose problems. For example, if yours is an old and grungy basement, you can create a darkened coffeehouse atmosphere that will be the perfect spot for poetry readings and impromptu entertainment.

However, a basement café tends to attract customers who are already using the library. Because the café is not readily visible, it does not act as a lure to bring in new customers.

Food service on your campus is probably the responsibility of an administrative department. It may require considerable skill and tact to convince the director of this department that a library café will not pose a threat or take business from existing facilities. For example, it may be possible for one of the student center's vendors to handle an expanded operation with an additional location in the library. If food service is outsourced, there may be clauses in existing contracts that prohibit additional facilities. Because the reasons why the library is considering a café have little to do with money, it probably does not matter that another department or vendor would take most of the profit. Just as long as bureaucratic conflicts are eliminated and the library covers its costs, your ends can be achieved. Nevertheless, it is important to retain some control over the operation. Since your goal is to bring additional customers to the library and enhance the experience of current customers, you will not want to compromise on the quality of the items sold. You will also want some control over the menu or you may find your library becoming a restaurant, with the library's activities taking second place. Neither the remains of chili left to molder in the stacks nor the smell of rancid cooking oil and hot dogs wafting through study areas are what you have in mind. This will require extensive discussion culminating in a written agreement.

Like other changes in the library, you will probably encounter some people who think a library should behave like a library. Sometimes it is simply a matter of educating your campus administrators about recent developments in libraries. They may have very traditional views of the library that just need to be updated. Although many libraries are currently operating successful cafés, it is true that this is new territory for libraries. Before getting too deeply involved, be sure to check out the impact a café might have on your library's electrical wiring, plumbing, and liability insurance. Have a heart-to-heart talk with your local health inspector and be sure you understand local regulations. The last thing the library needs is a case of food poisoning or a letter from a government agency demanding that you cease operations.

Popular Fiction/Leisure Reading Area

Academic libraries often find that popular fiction doesn't quite fit into their policies and procedures, so they may tend to avoid it. Yet such collections are often the most heavily used in the library, improving circulation statistics and making students feel at home. Even libraries on a tight budget can usually manage to create a cozy area with comfy lounge furniture, low bookcases, and perhaps table lamps that add warmth to an otherwise institutional-looking space. Remember, however, that the demographic profile of your customers is very different from that of a typical public library. Books about MySpace, cool vampires, or hip-hop will be a lot more popular than sophisticated novels aimed at middle-aged adults. Unlike most academic library resources, popular novels should be withdrawn when customers are no longer checking them out. You might, therefore, want to locate your popular fiction area near your café. Since you do not intend to keep these materials permanently, a coffee spill is a minor annoyance, not a major crisis. You may want to devise a temporary cataloging procedure that makes popular fiction easier to add to the collection and easier to withdraw.

Videoconferencing Room

Videoconferencing can play an important role in facilitating communication among students, faculty, university staff, and administrators, and even among the library staff. For example, students and faculty can hold meetings regardless of geographical barriers. Faculty can meet with their advisees, and expertise can be shared among students and faculty. The conferencing room will, of course, be very popular for distance learning courses, but it's probably best that it not be monopolized by your university's extended learning program. There are so many ways in which videoconferencing can enhance the image of the library and serve the needs of its customers that it's well worth holding on to the reins of this technology. Although bringing new customers into the library should be the primary reason for creating such a facility, it can also be extremely useful to the library staff. Your branch and central library staff members can attend the same meetings and committees and can work closely together even if they are on different sides of the campus or city or even in another state.

Commercial Copy Center

In many libraries, copy services have expanded beyond a few coin- or card-operated machines maintained by a reluctant library staff or by a mobile service staff who replace supplies a few times a week. Some libraries have invited commercial copy centers to set up branches in the library, staffing the center, collecting the profits, and perhaps paying the library a nominal rent.

Like the coffee shop, the library's real purpose in bringing in a copy center is to attract new library customers. The copy center shouldn't be viewed as a moneymaker, because the library's real concerns have more to do with quality of service and hours of operation. Both cafés and copy centers attract students, faculty, and staff who might never come to the library without the added incentive of a convenient service. Everyone needs to eat, and nearly everyone in the academic world occasionally needs to make a photocopy or bind a presentation. If the library provides services that compare favorably with other campus facilities, it will attract attention. Students may discover the library's existence and get into the library habit. As long as they're making a few photocopies, they might check out a book or view a DVD. Thus the library habit takes root. Of course, a commercial enterprise brings with it multiple questions and complications. What works for some libraries may not work for others, but the idea is definitely worth exploring.

Upscale Library Printing and Copying Services

If you're not quite ready for a full-service copy center, would it be a good idea to increase and upgrade the library's existing capability? Would your customers respond positively to more color copiers? Could you offer fax or scanner services? Would public computer users be willing to pay for color printouts? In fact, is it time to reconsider your copying charges? The actual cost of color printing and copying has gone down, but in many libraries you might think you were still living in 1995.

Information Kiosk

If you don't have the staff or the space for a fully functional information desk, why not create a small kiosk in the lobby area? It can be staffed with either students or regular staff. Volunteers may even be available, but they must be fully trained in the questions that customers commonly ask. If most of the library is invisible from the lobby, verbal directions may be of little use. Kiosk staff should also be willing to step outside the kiosk when necessary to escort customers to the reference librarian or point them toward the resources they need. Too many libraries that have tried the kiosk idea have seen it as a low priority and have left it unstaffed during busy periods. Once the decision is made to create a kiosk, it must be seen as a real commitment. Customers come to rely on the service, and the sight of the empty kiosk will give the impression of a library going rapidly downhill. If you really cannot spare even student staff, consider an electronic kiosk. It is essentially a computer housed in some type of cabinet and often includes a touch screen that allows customers to select choices without a mouse or keyboard. The kiosk is programmed to provide answers to customers' most common questions. Staff are still needed to check the machine a few times a day to be sure it is functioning properly, and it must be programmed to automatically return to the start or home page after a few minutes of inactivity.

On-Site, High-Density Storage

Something that frequently makes a library confusing and unattractive to students is a vast stack area stuffed with rarely used library materials. Finding what you are looking for can be like finding a needle in a haystack. Newer, more popular materials are surrounded by dusty tomes that may not have been checked out for ten years or more. If most of the books and other materials that students come across are musty, dusty, and dated, customers will decide that the library itself is musty, dusty, and dated. By moving these older materials to a high-density storage area, the library can become much more attractive and functional. Space will then become available for more popular resources and services. Compact shelving requires maintenance and may not be as convenient as regular shelving. It may need to be located on the ground floor or may require special building modifications to accommodate the additional weight. Nevertheless, the library will cease to resemble a warehouse and will take on a vibrant new look. Note that we're talking about on-site storage. Most librarians have found that locating such storage facilities off-site is counterproductive. Staff members must be assigned to maintain such a facility, thus making it necessary to sacrifice customer-service priorities.

Sharing Library Space

Many academic libraries are experiencing pressure to give up some of their space and surrender it to other campus departments. Consider carefully whether this is a battle you can win. Adding a popular café, a copy center, lounge, or learning center that attracts more customers may reduce pressure on the library. Nevertheless, if your personal analysis of the campus political environment indicates that this is an argument you may lose, why not take preemptive action? Partner with campus services that actually enhance the library and attract new customers. What campus offices or departments have goals that are complementary to those of the library? Which would not pose a threat to the library's independence?

You might suggest, for example, that your university press join you, because fact-checking editors will enjoy being near the resources they need. The editorial offices of academic presses are usually relatively small and don't take up a great deal of space. Prime library space, however, should not be used to meet their warehousing needs. How would the English department feel about such a move? Would academic advising or tutoring be a good match, or might it be the first step in an unwanted administrative reorganization? The point is that the library will be better off if it is able to choose its own tenants. If vast, rarely used stack areas have attracted the attention of covetous deans or department heads, then you will need to do something quickly. The old cliché "use it or lose it" clearly applies here. Filling the library with customers and making it a center of activity is the best defense against such dangers.

Lifelong Learning Center

Many colleges and universities deliberately set out to attract older, non-degree-seeking students. As the number of aging baby boomers swells, they are discovering that this is a population that is well worth reaching out to. Following up on the huge popularity of Elderhostel courses and other academic programs for boomers and seniors, they are devising educational experiences that are especially appealing to them. Members of this group are often avid students, and almost any course can catch their fancy. However, there are some that are especially popular. For example, retirees are intrepid travelers, and they enjoy preparing themselves for their trips. Conversational Spanish, Japanese, or Greek might allow older travelers to interact more personally with the people they meet. History classes also make their experiences more meaningful. Boomers and seniors want to know more about their own hometowns and regions, so local history and geology courses are attractive.

How can the library fit into their world? Such students are usually self-starters and discover many of the library's services and resources on their own. However, they may have difficulty reading small print, so a collection of large-print books, brighter lighting, and text magnification equipment are helpful. Macular degeneration can also interfere with their enjoyment of books and magazines. Such students, however, are different from younger visually impaired students in that their disability is of recent origin. They may be unfamiliar with the sophisticated technology that is available to them, so additional help may be needed. They may also feel that they are behind the curve when it comes to technology in general. Computer software programs that teach basic computer skills tend to be well used, and media programs that help them enjoy their hobbies and enhance their globetrotting experiences are also popular. Because these students enjoy getting to know one another, it's a good idea to provide spaces where small groups can view the same program, and you may even wish to schedule showings and workshops.

One of the most rewarding experiences I've ever had was teaching a computer workshop that was attended almost entirely by boomers and seniors. Although originally intended for traditional students, it inadvertently became almost a club for older students, senior university employees, and even retired faculty. Nothing I've ever done has given me more satisfaction. What began as a workshop became a permanent institution. Older faculty bonded with older students and helped them learn the ropes. Administrators shared their secrets for triumphing over the bureaucracy. A sixty-something student told me he had always thought of the university as a cold, impersonal place, but his on-campus life completely changed when he began attending the workshop. One eighty-year-old stroke survivor became extraordinarily skilled at using a computer to aid her recalcitrant memory. When I introduced my group to Google Earth, they made me feel that I had given them a priceless gift.

Graduate or Commuter Student Lounge

Because graduate students tend to spend more time in the library than undergraduates, why not give them a lounge of their own? Provide some comfortable furniture and maybe a refrigerator and a microwave oven. Get a committee of students together to help get the project organized and devise a few basic ground rules. If security is a concern, you can check out keys at the circulation desk, or students may have their own access cards. Just make sure students really feel welcome. On residential campuses, commuting students sometimes feel like second-class citizens. A commuters' lounge might be a good idea for them, and you might even consider starting a commuters club with a few additional perks that make them feel as if the library is their special place. Still another group that might appreciate a place of their own are your international students.

Teaching and Learning Center

Faculty members and graduate teaching assistants appreciate having a place where they can find support for their teaching: a place where they can get help with technology, produce visual aids, and check out media programs for class use. You might consider partnering with another campus department that works with faculty to create a center dedicated to improving the quality of instruction. Some library centers offer preview rooms where instructors can view films, videos, and DVDs. Others have teleconferencing facilities, media production labs, and other resources that help them improve their teaching skills and prepare their classes.

After-Hours Study Area

Sometimes called 24-hour areas, these are separate spaces provided so students can study after the library closes. Although they usually have a separate entrance and architectural barriers that limit access to other parts of the library, these study areas vary greatly in other respects. Consider how much of the library you can make available and still provide sufficient security protection. A barren, institutional-looking space will probably not attract anyone. Instead, you'll want to include inviting but hard-wearing decor, computers, a photocopy machine, an emergency phone, basic print resources, comfortable furniture, and, preferably, machines that dispense food and drink. There is nothing less appealing than an ugly, garishly lit room that looks as if it might be part of a prison or similar institution. When such facilities are poorly supervised or maintained, they repel rather than attract. I've seen many such spaces with large windows and bright lights that attract the attention of passersby with their ugliness and sense of desolation. They bring to mind the Edward Hopper painting of the all-night diner, certainly not the warm, congenial environment that appeals to students. Investing in a security guard who can also provide basic library services, equipping the space as you would most other library areas, and adding high-end fast-food machines can transform such spaces into welcoming, well-used, all-night libraries. Twenty-four-hour areas are usually available only to students and faculty, so think about how you will limit access. Card readers are common, or a security guard might personally check identification before allowing customers to enter.

Many libraries find that they must choose between an insecure 24-hour area and an adequately staffed extended-hours facility that is open fewer hours. You may discover that you serve more customers and serve them better by limiting hours. Students will not use a facility they consider unsafe. Some locations are safer than others, but colleges and universities that merely rely on campus security to walk through the area now and then lose many potential users. Consider a student questionnaire to help determine the most desirable time periods. Not many students are really studying at 4:00 a.m., but you might find that you have a full house at midnight.

If you have the opportunity to design or renovate an information commons, you might consider separating part of it with glass partitions and making it available after hours. Many academic libraries find that most late-night users are primarily interested in access to computers.

Collaborative Study Rooms

If you have stayed abreast of recent trends in teaching and learning, you know that collaborative learning has gained rapidly in popularity. Students may prefer to work together simply because they enjoy one another's company, because they are working with a tutor, or because they are working on a collaborative assignment. Either way, they need enclosed, nonclaustrophobic spaces where they have helpful tools like whiteboards and where their conversation will not bother other library users. Students working on a project often need to access a website or watch a DVD. They will be much more productive if they can view these resources together without having to trek across the library to the multimedia area or computer lab. That way they can interact with the media, pausing to discuss the content and sharing ideas as they occur. Large windows or window walls assure that they are also safe from library predators.

Used Bookstore

A small used bookstore can be an attractive and popular service to customers, or it can be merely an annoying burden to the library staff. A bookstore provides an opportunity to sell unwanted library donations and discards, but it requires care and attention. You might create a volunteer group or identify a student service club that is looking for a fund-raising project and turn the bookstore over to them. Let them keep the proceeds. The books will find good homes and the library will enjoy the positive publicity without having to use library staff members to keep the store open. Locating the bookstore near the café may increase sales and help protect the library's own collection. Make sure that you have a clear agreement with the group specifying that the area will be kept in order and will be open at least a specified number of hours. If the group loses interest, your hands should not be tied, and another group may be delighted to earn a little extra income.

Music-Listening Room

For many years, libraries have grudgingly provided individual "closets" or booths where students could listen to recordings assigned in their music classes. Some of these spaces were so claustrophobic that they were occupied only when students had no other options available. If you are in the process of renovating your library or planning an addition, you might wish to consider soundproofing some collaborative study rooms so students can play both assigned and personal music. Many students believe that they study better surrounded by sound, so set up the sound system so they can plug in their iPods or bring their own CDs. Music classes still depend on the library, but you can also make it possible for students to listen to music of their own choosing.

Adaptive Technology Lab

Many libraries have purchased a few high-tech machines intended for students with visual impairments and believe that they are serving the needs of their disabled customers. Of course, the staff often fail to publicize the availability of the equipment or master its operation, so it gathers dust. Most universities and colleges have an organization for people with disabilities. Staff might attend some of their meetings and encourage the group to work closely with the library, designing a technology space they will really use. Of course, this means real commitment from the staff, but it's one of the services that can actually change lives.

Although an adaptive technology lab is a wonderful addition, remember that people with disabilities need to use the whole library. In fact, a new lab will attract new customers who will then feel comfortable and want to explore more of the library's resources. Once again, it is real people with disabilities who can best suggest ways to make the library more accessible.

A "Happening" Place

Make some room for a small performance space. One library director I visited saw the handwriting on the wall when the library discarded most of its bound journals. A roving university administrator happened upon the empty stacks and immediately began asking probing questions. It was clear that she had plans for the space. Quick as a wink, the Machiavellian library director replied that the area was being redesigned as a performance space. Shamefacedly, he confessed his fib at the next librarians' meeting, but instead of boos, the idea was met with enthusiasm. As it happened, the library had always enjoyed a close relationship with the performing arts departments, and what began as a hasty ploy became a successful cooperative venture. You too might want to invite performing arts departments to use the space for student recitals and one-act plays. Set Friday nights aside for student rock bands and folksingers. Invite area artists to give concerts. Schedule visiting writers to read from their work. Ask faculty to present their more popular lectures. Another academic library has set aside a space the size of a small classroom and mounted a large flat-screen TV on the wall. Comfortably padded chairs accommodate approximately twenty people. Because scheduling audiovisual equipment for classroom use is somewhat complicated for teaching faculty members, they are encouraged to bring their classes over for a video or DVD showing. When major news events are in progress, the television is turned to CNN. Customers sit down for a few moments, catch up on the latest information, and then go on to class.

Japanese Garden

A New England library director worried that her library was dark and uninviting. In winter it was especially bleak. When she managed to obtain funds for a renovation project, she decided to do something daring. She took part of the space that had previously housed bound periodicals and turned it into a garden room. She supplemented the skylight with full-spectrum fluorescents and enhanced the effect with pale, butter yellow walls. Lots of bamboo and other plants, a very small pond complete with motorized waterfall, low tables, a few Japanese accessories, and piles of floor cushions completed the decor. A company was hired at a surprisingly reasonable cost to provide the plants and maintain them. Students began flocking to the garden as soon as the carpenters left, and the space continues to be the most popular in the library. The library director is now talking about an adjoining Japanese tea garden instead of the usual café.

Media Production Lab

Many instructors no longer assign lengthy research papers but, instead, require their students to produce some type of media program to be presented in class. In addition, many of their collaborative assignments also involve a media component, whether a video program, a website, or a PowerPoint presentation. Some of these programs can be created on the library's public computers, but others require access to more sophisticated equipment or materials. Libraries can sometimes integrate a facility that library staff members use to create their own instructional videos, slide shows, and presentations with a production lab for faculty and students.

Such facilities, however, cannot usually be left unstaffed. Sophisticated equipment can be easily damaged, and nearly every library worries about theft and vandalism. If you don't have staff available to monitor a multimedia production lab, consider lockable multimedia cabinets, each of which contains the equipment needed for a specific type of project. Check out keys to the cabinets at the circulation desk. Although this isn't an ideal solution, it may meet most of the needs of your customers. You may want to offer workshops in production techniques and use workshop attendance to identify the students, faculty, and library staff members qualified to use the equipment. A docking station makes it easier to connect personal laptop computers with library-owned peripheral equipment like scanners and graphics tablets.

Student Learning Centers

These are high-tech classrooms that can be used for a wide variety of functions, including information literacy classes, workshops, collaborative study groups, lectures, and other library gatherings. Because the library can usually offer better security for expensive equipment than most classroom buildings, library learning centers can offer high-tech equipment that is unavailable elsewhere. This means that teaching faculty will want to reserve the space for their classes. This is a great way to bring both faculty and students to the library, but be sure that the library puts its own stamp on the center.

Telephone Center

Instead of constantly playing the heavy with signs banning cell phones, why not create a comfortable, attractive place where students can make and take their calls? Although we assume that all students are joined to cell phones like extra bodily appendages, students of limited means may not be able to afford the monthly charges for such phones. Be sure to provide a couple of pay phones in the telephone center to serve their needs.

ENHANCING LIBRARY SERVICES

While many of the innovative ideas that are sweeping through the academic library community require new space or new uses for existing space, some simply enhance existing library spaces, making it possible for them to better serve the needs of library customers. Here are a few possibilities.

Library-wide Wireless Networks

This idea is closely related to the information commons, but it encompasses the entire library. Students can retreat to the farthermost corners of the library and still be able to use their laptop computers. We would much prefer that students spend their time in the library than in some other campus building or off-campus coffee shop. Wireless connectivity is a great inducement for a modest investment. A buildingwide wireless network is relatively inexpensive, since it is not necessary to install miles of cabling. However, laptop battery charges are short-lived, so most students will want to plug their computers into electrical outlets.

Rethinking Service Desks

In chapters 2 and 3, we discussed the changing roles of the library staff. Some libraries have consolidated service desks because of budget cuts or because they believed that staff could be better utilized. However, such decisions have often had a negative impact on customer service. Why not take a broader look at service desks and how they are used by your customers? Are there strategies that would allow staff to be available to the public and yet productively occupied with other library duties during slower periods? Are service desks conveniently located? In other words, are they located in areas where customers most often need help or encounter problems? It may be that you can provide more service points or increase the functionality of existing service points without sacrificing other library priorities.

Circulating Digital Cameras

Digital cameras are no longer just expensive toys, and a serviceable camera can be purchased at a cost of roughly one hundred dollars. Multimedia assignments often require students to create their own images. Although they may own digital cameras, they probably don't bring them to campus. The ability to borrow cameras from the library means that students can use their time more effectively, working on assignments when it is most convenient. It also means that students with limited means have the same opportunities as more affluent students. Although some camera models are too delicate and breakable for public use, many are built to survive rough handling. Try to examine the camera you are considering. Avoid ones with small plastic bits and pieces that can easily break or fall off. Manuals tend to get lost, so the more intuitive the camera's operation the better.

Enhanced Lobby

Just as retail stores place their most eye-catching displays near the front door, libraries can use a similar "come-hither" approach. Add a popular books nook near the entrance or place a few paperback racks where they can be seen by entering students. Create a lounge area where customers can pause, browse through some paperbacks, and revive their spirits. Customers might also view a slide show introduction to the library while they're recharging their batteries.

Speed-Read E-mail Stations

Students on their way to class may want to stop briefly to check their e-mail messages. Placing a few stand-up computer workstations near the entrance has proven to be very popular in many academic libraries. Just as a lounge area or paperback rack beckons to tired students, the chance to communicate with friends exerts a similar attraction.

THE INNOVATIVE LIBRARY STAFF

Making changes in the library building and creating new spaces to accommodate new services cannot be done in isolation. No new space or service can be successful without the support and expertise of the library staff. The following are some changes that you might wish to consider.

Step Out of the Box

As we all know, the term *librarian* continues to be associated with silly stereotypes and assumptions in the minds of many of our customers. If you doubt that librarians are still seen as frumpy, bespectacled, and out of touch with contemporary life, find an opportunity to view Ann Seidl's wonderful film *The Hollywood Librarian*. Although it is a somewhat superficial approach, a change of titles can sometimes cause faculty and students to view us differently. The titles "knowledge analyst," "informationist," and "project information specialist" may seem a little silly, but you might want to experiment with some new titles that capture the attention of your users and possibly force them to take another look at our profession.

Embed Librarians into Online Courses

Increasingly, college and university courses are being delivered over the Internet using software modules called "courseware." It is possible to embed or insert librarians into academic courses by transporting them into cyberspace. Librarians may be unofficially enrolled as students, not in the course but in the software program. Courseware may also allow them to function as guest lecturers. Library participation can take the form of a "library" discussion folder or thread, making it possible for students to chat with or message the librarian. The librarian, in turn, can post suggestions for particular assignments and can contribute whatever information literacy–focused additions are appropriate.

Create a Multimedia Team

Many librarians and other staff members are somewhat reluctant to create multimedia programs. Although there is ample evidence that point-of-use slide shows and other instructive programs can greatly enhance the customer's library experience, they can be intimidating to the fledgling program creator. Why not bring together the library's most media-sophisticated staff members? Make them responsible for increasing the quantity and improving the quality of library media programs. They might offer workshops or work individually with staff members. In addition, you might want to make use of their more sophisticated skills and give them the job of producing the library's more heavily used programs as a collaborative effort.

Assign Library Staff Members to Classroom Buildings

Why not turn a small office desk into a "branch library"? Send a librarian or other staff member to work part of their day in a classroom building with computers that can access the library's OPAC and journal databases. Set up an efficient document delivery system that encourages students and faculty to identify, request, pick up, and return materials at these remote service points.

Be sure staff members assigned to the remote service point have access to the library's circulation and interlibrary loan modules. That way they can charge and discharge materials as well as request items on interlibrary loan. Even small reserve collections can be remotely maintained, and electronic reserves can be accessed from anywhere. It is important too that roving staff members spend part of their time working in the library. That way they identify with their peers and can better act as liaisons between the library and its users. Instant messaging between the reference desk and remote service points can also help maintain a sense of "togetherness."

You might, for example, wish to create a remote service point and assign a library staff member to the nursing department. Nursing tends to be a department of very active library users. The personal attention made possible by a library service desk may increase their library use dramatically. Again, it is important that staff members spend part of their work schedule in the library so that they don't lose their identities as library staff members. Remember that in this uncertain time for academic libraries, you must make it clear to decision makers that these are library services. Brag about them whenever possible; include them in library statistics, distribute library marketing materials at remote sites, and hang big signs over remote service desks that read "Library" in big, bold letters.

Offer Computer Workshops for Nontraditional Students

Students and faculty over the age of forty probably grew up without personal computers in their homes. When computers became more common, they may have avoided them whenever possible, limiting their use to e-mail and word processing. There is no question that most students will be more successful if they develop good computer skills, and faculty members will be more effective in their jobs if they learn how computers can impact their teaching. Older customers may be reluctant to admit their weaknesses because it seems as if the high-tech world has passed them by. Getting small groups of older faculty and students together in a relaxed, comfortable environment can be a very rewarding experience.

Team-Teach Courses with Faculty

One of the hallmarks of a really effective information literacy program is flexibility. Teaching faculty tend to use the library differently depending on the discipline. Librarians teaching information literacy classes and workshops may not really understand these differences among faculty members. When teaching faculty are paired with librarians, however, both come to understand one another's worlds. Students leave class understanding how the library can be an integral part of almost any academic endeavor.

Make Student Workers More Responsible

Training and supervising student assistants is one of the most important keys to library success. It seems to be a fact of human nature that we throw ourselves into our work when we feel a sense of personal responsibility for the success of an endeavor. When we feel no personal responsibility, we may not exert ourselves. It's difficult to create individual roles for each student worker, but they will be far more effective if their responsibilities are clear. When something doesn't get done, an individual, not a group, should be responsible. When it is possible to assign responsibility for one small section of the library, students can be especially effective. For example, within their small kingdoms, they may staff a small service point, shelve and dust materials, pick up trash, and assist customers. In addition, they may gather up materials for customers who call in or e-mail their requests. This way, busy customers can stop by a service desk, pick up needed materials, and be on their way. Such arrangements require considerable planning and training, but they can generate a great deal of positive public approval.

Assign Roving Staff Members to Assist Customers

When you shop at high-end retail stores, you are frequently asked whether you're finding what you're looking for. If you are, indeed, looking for something in particular, the answer is often "yes." Occasionally this can become a little excessive, but you will usually have a more positive feeling about the store if its staff are concerned about your needs. Such helpfulness can also save you a lot of time and increase the chances that you'll find the skirt or air purifier that you were seeking. In a similar way, roving staff members are often the first to identify a problem in the library. They may discover it themselves or customers may notify them. Roving reference librarians have been popular in library literature, but any fully trained public service staff member can be successful. And don't forget that godsend to library customers, the roving technician.

Create a Friends of the Library Group

As has been mentioned repeatedly, the library staff has shrunk while library space has grown. Friends of the Library groups, traditionally associated with public libraries, can be even more effective in academic libraries. Why not recruit volunteers to staff an additional information desk or rove the library equipped with cell phones and large buttons reading "How can I help?"

Fund-raising is a traditional function of Friends groups, but expanding and enhancing the presence of the library staff can be even more helpful. They can give directions, report problems, and generally create the impression of a much more visible library staff.

Create a Grad Student Help Line

Not everyone possesses the skills to satisfy the needs of grad students. Consider how the library can personalize their experience, keeping them connected with staff members who understand their needs and are experienced in meeting them. Assign a small group of staff members the task of maintaining a grad student telephone help line. Make the service available on the library's website and use a chat room program or instant messaging to make it possible for students to access the service from any location. Assigning grad students their own personal librarian is another great idea.

Rethink Evening and Weekend Staffing

Most library staff members work only during standard business hours. This means that most of the staff available to assist customers at other times are student workers. Each academic library has different usage patterns, but many actually serve more customers when fewer staff members are working. This means that customers may be largely unaware of the quality of service that regular staff can provide. They may assume that there is no reason to pay for a large and highly qualified library staff when students do all the work anyway. In most cases, it is possible to redistribute staff hours more evenly. Are there staff members who can be assigned some additional evening and weekend hours? If it is simply a matter of personal preferences standing in the way of quality library service, you're doing your customers a grave disservice.

FINE-TUNING LIBRARY SERVICES

Because it is becoming clear that traditional library services like book circulation are in decline, it is important for librarians to consider what services their customers really want. The following are some new services that are being implemented in many academic libraries.

Student Websites on Library Computer Servers

Many universities and colleges allow students to maintain websites on their central servers. Equip some library computers with web authoring software so that customers can work on their websites between classes. Remember, however, that the students most likely to take advantage of this opportunity are the less experienced ones. They will probably need help, so the library staff will need to understand the basics of website design.

One library that received a more enthusiastic response to the service than it could accommodate set up a series of workshops for aspiring webmasters. To obtain passwords needed to access the authoring software, students were required to attend one of the workshops.

Service to Distance Education Programs

Because many colleges and universities are expanding their distance education programs and many students earn their degrees primarily through the Internet, an excellent opportunity exists to expand the library's services. Yet distance education students usually go largely unserved by the library. Occasionally, we make arrangements with a public library or local community college to provide a few reserve materials or mail a few boxes of books to the instructor. Perhaps there's a note on the library's website that encourages distance learners to contact the library. Real service to these customers involves a great deal more than this, however.

In a section earlier in this chapter, we discussed the idea of embedding librarians into courses, whether traditional ones or those beamed electronically to remote students. There are other ways to serve your institution's distant learning population that can be just as effective. Remember that distant students are isolated. They lack the daily interaction with their instructors and fellow students that on-site students enjoy. They must interpret their readings, assignments, and other learning activities in isolation. What may seem perfectly obvious to a traditional student may cause the distant student hours of frustration.

Imagine, however, that a librarian or library liaison is always available via instant messaging. Distant students also tend to be nontraditional students, adults who have been in the workforce for a number of years and now need to upgrade their skills. This means that they may be less sophisticated computer users, but instant messaging programs are among the easiest to learn. Imagine that when they have a question, a caring library staff member is available to respond, elucidating the mysteries of the OPAC, tracking down a journal article that is supposed to be on electronic reserve, and discussing the resources available for research paper topics. Careful scheduling can make it possible for some staff member to always be available to respond to messages. It is important that students feel they have a friend and mentor in the library. This means letting them know when their favorite librarian will be available and even sending them e-mail messages from time to time to see how they're doing.

When "Self-Service" Means "Better Service"

Most academic libraries are increasing the number of library services that do not require the intervention of staff members. For example, customers can charge out their own materials at self-checkout stations, renew them from their home computers, request interlibrary loans, and view their records online. Customers appreciate the ability to take charge of their own library interactions, but there's a downside. By removing personal interaction with the library staff, you increase the perception among students and faculty that the library is merely a warehouse staffed by all but invisible warehouse clerks. As librarians, we want students to understand that research is an activity that demands a high level of skill. Research is far more than the ability to query Google, and it requires some understanding of the organization of knowledge. Librarians are expert researchers who are happy to share their education and experience.

Each time the library makes it possible for customers to perform a function without assistance from the library staff, be aware that it means one less interaction with that same library staff, one less opportunity for communication. Consider how you will replace this lost interaction. Staffing funds have been freed up, because library personnel are no longer needed to perform these routine tasks. Why not use these newly available funds to provide more meaningful customer interaction?

Using Cable and Public TV to Market the Library

Many colleges and universities broadcast programs on their own TV station, often as an adjunct to an academic communications department. Some stations are almost never viewed outside the departments that sponsor them. However, many serve as the local PBS station, with powerful transmitters that broadcast the signal long distances, and are included in standard cable TV packages. If your college or university station reaches a large number of students, it may be worthwhile to create a library-literacy television program. Be forewarned, however, that a high-quality program requires a lot of work. If you have a good relationship with the broadcasting department and if you can hire broadcasting majors as student workers, you may find it well worth the effort. A radio program might be a better choice if these resources are unavailable. Try to choose interesting topics and avoid excessive "how-to" detail. Unless the library's program will be incorporated into academic courses, it must have considerable entertainment value to attract viewers.

As you've been reading this chapter, you've probably been thinking that this or that idea sounds impractical and definitely wouldn't work in your library. Your college or university doesn't have its own radio or TV station, or your staff couldn't be stretched thin enough to provide an additional service. We are surrounded by people, especially high-level university administrators, who have no idea how costly and labor-intensive it is to operate a library. Over time, we've become defensive when we're confronted with "bright ideas" proposed by people who rarely set foot in the library. For the moment, however, try to silence that defensive voice. Turn up the volume of your creative voice that is saying, "Maybe if we tweaked this job description and pulled a few dollars from that budget line, we could . . ." When we begin listening to that voice, all sorts of things are possible.

RESOURCES

Acker, Stephen R., and Michael D. Miller. "Campus Learning Spaces: Investing in How Students Learn." *EDUCAUSE Research Bulletin* 2005, no. 8 (April 12, 2005). EDUCAUSE Center for Applied Research.

Association of Research Libraries. "Service Trends in ARL Libraries, 1991–2003." In *ARL Statistics 2002–03*. Washington, DC: Association of Research Libraries, 2004. Available at www.arl.org/stats/arlstat/graphs/2003/pubser03 .pdf.

Oblinger, Diana. "Boomers, Gen-Xers, and Millennials: Understanding the New Students." *EDUCAUSE Review* 38, no. 4 (July/August 2003). Available at www.educause.edu/ir/library/pdf/ERM0342.pdf.

7

INNOVATION AT THE FOREFRONT

During the last decade, the concept of an information commons has been enthusiastically embraced by librarians across the length and breadth of the academic landscape. As mentioned in the last chapter, the commons in earlier times was a piece of land that was used by the community as a whole. The thought of an entire academic community sharing a sophisticated technology space and sharing resources that would not otherwise be available is an extremely appealing one. Commons areas vary greatly from one library to another, but, in theory, they are inviting places where the academic community is encouraged to find, use, and create information.

DESIGNING THE INFORMATION COMMONS

Essentially, the information commons allows individual students to use hardware, software, and other electronic resources in a pleasant, convenient place where help is readily available. Students can use equipment that they would probably be unable to afford and can avail themselves of the human, print, and media-based assistance needed to use it effectively. Because so many different kinds of resources, including trained staff, are available in one place, the commons can support projects all the way from conception to completion. Because the commons is traditionally a place where people can come together, collaboration and consultation are important considerations in its design. Groups can meet together to collaborate on projects using furniture configurations and software specifically designed to accommodate them. At this point, most larger universities offer their students something resembling an information commons, and even smaller institutions are well on the way to creating similar but smaller-scale facilities.

The Customer's Point of View

Imagine for a moment a group of students designing a library technology center. In fact, you might imagine them designing an entire technology-friendly library. They would, of course, begin with their own needs. They would imagine themselves working within their own world on their own projects. Library resources could be useful and relevant if they could be readily imported into this personal world, a world that exists, to a large extent, on their own computers.

Before we consider the kind of facility that students might design, let's pause for a moment and consider facilities they would not design and would not even want to visit. For example, they would not design a computer lab. Nor would they imitate some librarians I've known by hanging a sign reading "Information Commons" above the computer lab and consider their work done. Computer labs have been around since academic institutions first began making computers available to their students. In technology terms, this was a long, long time ago, and the basic concept has changed little in the intervening years. A computer lab usually consists of a lot of desks or tables squashed together, accommodating a line of desktop computers. Labs provided an easy way of managing (and policing) a large number of computers. They were often used as classrooms, so squeezing a lot of students and a lot of equipment into a small space was important. Every computer was usually identical to every other computer and was set up to be used in precisely the same way. Of course, that was the way instructors preferred it. Besides, early personal computers had extremely limited capabilities, so, to some extent, this uniformity reflected the state of technology twenty-five years ago. However, even in that bygone era, the one-size-fits-all setup of the typical computer lab shouted intolerance.

Take my experience, for example. I am completely and utterly left-handed. I don't have an ambidextrous bone in my body. However, I have always held a computer mouse in my right hand. That's because the computer labs of my youth were inflexible. Users were forbidden to "mess up" or change the computers in any way. The small space allotted to the mouse pad was always on the right, the mouse itself was designed for right-handed use, and the mouse buttons could be comfortably depressed only by people using their right hand. I probably had as much difficulty forcing my recalcitrant right hand to function as I did learning SPSS. I couldn't begin to count the errors I made simply by pressing the wrong button or accidentally deleting a calculation. If you were to look closely at most of today's computer labs, you would probably discover similarly intolerant planning at work.

Because computer labs were designed for one activity and one activity alone, desks did not provide space for textbooks, notepads, or even for students who were squashed together like sardines. They have always been places that must be uncomfortably endured, and yet libraries have included untold numbers of computer labs in their buildings. My experience visiting a large number of academic libraries has confirmed that somewhat expanded and perhaps slightly more comfortable computer labs are alive and well. Computers are still being squeezed into small areas of the library, apparently to make them easier to supervise and to save money on power and data upgrades. While perhaps 80 percent of library space is only sparsely populated by customers, the computer area is always uncomfortably full. Even though we have plenty of experience with the habits of our student users, we design spaces in which we know they will be uncomfortable. Think about the way students like to spread out. Instead, they must juggle the library's printed resources as well as their own notes and photocopies while working clumsily at the library's desktop computers. If they have their own laptops, the desks become even more crowded, and that still leaves the problem of backpacks and purses. I recently visited a library with a small, crowded information commons née computer lab and found myself watching one particular student sitting in front of a desktop computer. Books were piled in stacks at her feet, and her backpack had been accidentally kicked under her neighbor's desk. When she moved her chair, the stacks of books cascaded around her, disturbing several students working nearby. She was forced to get down on her knees, retrieve the books, pile them once again in stacks, and then attempt to retrieve her train of thought.

Planning the Information Commons

While I'm on the subject of my visits to academic libraries, I cannot help mentioning one particular information commons that has been repeatedly touted in library literature. Not one but two members of the planning group for this commons successfully milked the experience to produce journal articles and to support their respective tenure quests. The planning process took place over a two-year period and required frequent meetings attended by a large proportion of the professional library staff and various campus representatives. They produced well-written and professional-looking interim reports and a very extensive final report before actual work on the project commenced. In other words, the talents of a number of highly trained professionals were pooled to produce what should have been an unusually successful plan. Yet what they actually produced was an expensive but inadequate computer lab. The project participants completely failed to anticipate the number of potential users, specifying somewhat more equment than could be housed in the typical classroom lab of a quarter century ago. The equipment was top of the line and the furniture was both attractive and expensive. The computer desks were more spacious, but, overall, they had simply redesigned an anachronism.

Of course, I was not able to eavesdrop on the committee meetings, but we have all participated in enough meetings to make some educated guesses about what might have gone wrong. I had the additional advantage of being able to interview a few of the participants. Because representation in the group was broad, a number of members knew very little about computers, and their views sometimes carried more weight than others who possessed more sophisticated computer expertise. Neither the token student nor the faculty member on the committee attended many meetings, probably because they were bored with the long discussions and occasional infighting. When conflicts arose, the chair sought to bring the group together by eliminating controversial elements of the project. Almost no cost comparisons were performed, so the funds available did not begin to cover the kind of project originally envisioned. Although inexperienced members tended to equate quality with high prices, one more technically savvy member kept throwing in expensive "toys" that he himself would enjoy playing with.

How Customers Use Computers and Computer Programs

Most groups planning an information commons facility make a serious effort to get input from students and faculty. They often develop questionnaires, learn what software programs are being used in which classes, and generally accept the importance of listening to voices outside the library. Up to a point, these efforts are useful and necessary. However, they tend to focus on what, not how. In other words, when the results of questionnaires are tabulated, the output is a list of software programs and hardware specifications. What is missing is a sense of how customers, usually students, will really use the commons in their day-to-day activities.

Suppose the imaginary student designers we consulted above were presented with a typical information commons and asked their opinion. "Well, yes, those flat-screen monitors are great. The high-speed desktop computers are fine too. But you have a sign on them that says 'No Downloading.' What good are they if I can't keep the articles I find?" Another student might complain: "My laptop battery is low. I don't see any electric outlets." In my experience, student focus groups are most likely to produce this kind of information, but only when they're presented with the right questions. Take, for example, a graduate student who needs a sophisticated statistical package. A questionnaire would probably elicit only the information that the program is needed by certain students in certain classes. But how does this student use the program? Is it likely that another version of the program is loaded on her desktop computer at home? Does she copy her files from one computer to the other? Is she an experienced user, or has she received little or no training? Is the data she will input into the program available on the Internet, or will she be carrying around stacks of paper? Is the data archive freely available, or should the library make special arrangements for student access?

Although faculty questionnaires may leave the impression that students will be using a large number of complicated programs, it usually turns out that the basic, plain-vanilla applications are most in demand. Because the information commons is intended to serve the needs of the entire academic community, it must be prepared for both highly sophisticated computer users and for beginners whose experience does not extend beyond basic e-mail and word processing. Whether dealing with newbie or veteran, the library's goal is to make it possible for each and every customer to be productive and successful. This means that the kind of assistance provided by the library must meet a wide variety of different needs.

The Help We Provide

The information commons, however, is an excellent place to make available high-end software that might be too costly for purchase by individual departments. Such programs may be highly specialized, complicated, and difficult to use. How can a relatively small staff assist customers with so many programs? It really isn't possible for the staff to become advanced users of every program available on library computers. Nevertheless, students rely on the library staff and will assume they can help. The solution must inevitably be a compromise. Each time the library invests in a new software program, it has a responsibility to anticipate the way students will use it and the problems they might encounter.

Help comes in several forms, including tutorials that accompany programs, handbooks, DVD-based instructional programs, online help, and, of course, knowledgeable human beings. A combination of these resources should be close at hand if the information commons is to serve its purpose. However, only a human being possesses the flexibility to diagnose the need and prescribe the right remedy. This does not mean that staff members assigned to the commons must understand the intricacies of SPSS. However, they can and should do what librarians have always done so well. Whether we look to Ranganathan or Melvil Dewey, one of our most important responsibilities is to match the reader with the book, the appropriate book or tutorial that will satisfy his or her unique needs. While an experienced computer user might find the answer to her questions in a software manual, that same manual might seem to the beginning user to be written in gibberish.

Because this responsibility has been stressed for so long by so many, one would think that librarians are extremely well qualified to satisfy the information needs of their computer users, but when one looks at the print and multimedia resources available in many information commons, that assumption does not seem to be well founded. I made a point, as I was visiting different commons facilities, to note the programs (including versions) available on the computers. Then I went off in search of the appropriate manuals and tutorials that students might need to use the programs effectively. In some cases, I found no attempt whatsoever to provide software-support materials within the commons area. If, for example, the library owned copies of the popular "Dummies" handbooks, they were shelved in the stacks far away from the commons, and sometimes I found them checked out. More often, there was some effort made to provide printed resources within the commons, but it was a halfhearted effort at best. For example, I often found that a new version of a software program had been installed, but the manual or handbook for the old version was the only one available.

Commons Equipment Costs

While visiting one academic library, I was allowed to examine the equipment budget for a recently remodeled information commons. What startled me was the cost of standard, what you might call "garden-variety" PCs. In general, it is not particularly difficult to select computers. One looks for a company with a good track record, including readily available technical support, an up-to-date operating system, large hard drives, generous RAM, high speed, and a reputation for sturdy, long-lived components. Then most people would compare prices. Of course, more complicated installations involve other considerations, but most users are accessing the Internet, using Microsoft Office, or working with discipline-specific software that has no unusual hardware requirements.

It seemed to me that, like the planning group described above, the group that planned this particular information commons did not consider cost carefully enough. Because higher unit costs reduced the amount of equipment that could be purchased, the redesigned area was always crowded, and students often waited until a computer was available. In fact, the cost of these computers was almost twice what it might have been had the planning group done some serious comparison shopping. I inquired about any special restrictions or limitations in their freedom to make selections, but apparently none existed. From the various reports produced by the group, it was clear that they had spent quite a bit of time investigating equipment and had even created impressive tables comparing features.

Let's be somewhat conservative and assume that the group might have purchased half again the number of basic computers with the same amount of money. If they actually purchased 40 computers, they might have purchased 60; if they purchased 80, they might have purchased 120, and so on. This means that half again the number of customers could have been accommodated. Half again the number of customers would have had a more successful library experience. If the planning group had made its selections carefully, it's difficult to see how they could have gone wrong. Reliability, of course, must be an important concern, but many computer brands get high marks on dependability. Perhaps they might have had to sacrifice a few gigabytes of hard drive space, but often no such sacrifice is necessary. I'm afraid that one of the characteristics that sometimes makes committee decisions less than successful is a kind of perfectionism that can blind committee members to their real purpose. For example, in this case, planners must have understood that the commons would be very popular, so accommodating a large number of users would clearly be a priority. Student need certainly should have trumped a few minor bells and whistles, but in reading over the reports, that issue does not seem to have been an important consideration.

State-of-the-Art Technology

A number of years ago, I made a bad mistake. The computer technicians in my library were very enthusiastic about a new type of computer. Actually, that's a huge understatement, because they were ecstatic about the computer. It appeared to solve many of the problems we were having, and I failed to raise any substantive objections. What I learned the hard way was that there's a great deal to be said for standardization. It turned out that the marvelous computers were more or less what they claimed to be (not marvelous but not monstrous either), but they caused endless problems. That was because the rest of the world didn't know or care about our computers. We were overwhelmed with the constant frustration of doing everything differently from the way other libraries, other university departments, and other technicians were doing it. Compatibility with other technology was naturally a problem, as was procuring replacement parts and technical help on issues beyond the scope of our in-house staff. Gradually, the wonder computers were phased out to everyone's relief, but we had lost an opportunity to move another step forward in our technology plan. Had we simply purchased the computers that everyone else was buying at the time, even if they weren't wonderful, we would have been much better stewards of our institution's money.

Libraries (I say this so often that I know I sound like a broken record) are nearly all underfunded. I wouldn't say we're exactly poor, but counting our pennies is an important responsibility. We cannot afford bleeding-edge technology. No matter how attractive it might be, we must let the for-profit world with its deep pockets take most of the risk. In visiting different information commons, I found elaborate installations with equipment that was once state of the art. I don't know why it was purchased. Perhaps a faculty member said that the library must provide this or that capability for his students. Perhaps a member of the planning team was wowed by an article in a computer magazine. Whatever the reason for its purchase, the workstations were rarely used. When designing the information commons, it is essential to consult with faculty, especially those in science and technology. However, they must not view the library as Santa Claus, and planners have a responsibility to be on the lookout for requests that look more like letters to Santa than reasonable recommendations.

Security versus Utility

As you are planning an information commons facility, be sure to involve some highly skilled systems administrators. To obtain the needed expertise, you may have to go beyond the library staff and possibly even beyond the college or university. The point is that you need people who are able to "think outside the box," and entry-level technicians usually do not possess this kind of flexibility. One of the reasons such sophisticated expertise is necessary is security. Every technology facility must grapple with the dual priorities of functionality and security. Whenever I read professional articles in computer journals, I inevitably come across the belief that the average computer user is a menace. Technicians are advised to view their users as dangerous idiots who will inevitably engage in risky practices and bring their systems down if they are not kept under tight control.

This philosophy recommends that when setting up an individual computer or a network, technicians should begin by denying users all rights except those acknowledged to be essential. Of course, they usually don't understand what computer users will be doing and, therefore, don't really know what is essential. When, let's say, office workers discover that they can't do what they want to do, their outcry usually results in somewhat more flexible network settings. Although this strategy wastes a great deal of time, it can be minimally acceptable. It is, however, a totally unacceptable policy for an information commons. Although security problems in public technology facilities are numerous, technicians simply cannot depend on this method for assigning rights and privileges.

A few years ago, a student in my own library commons had a problem using a feature in Microsoft Office. The student worker who was the first on the scene was unable to resolve it, so she alerted a staff member, who in turn called in a technician. It should have been a fairly simple matter, but somehow none of the staff members could resolve the problem. Finally, the computer manager was tracked down and escorted to the troublesome computer. "Of course, you can't use that feature." His tone made it clear that any idiot should have known this. "It's a security violation." As we all know, technical staff and traditional library staff do not always live together in peace and harmony, and this incident turned out to be the straw that broke the camel's back. The particular function in question wasn't absolutely necessary, but it was certainly useful.

Meeting followed meeting, and it was quickly discovered that the manager had made a number of potentially controversial, security-related decisions, and he sometimes failed to share them with even his own technical staff. He clearly held the view that computer users are dangerous and need to be restrained. With security his only priority, the manager made what he thought were perfectly obvious decisions, the basis for which anyone should understand. Although some of these decisions did, indeed, turn out to be essential to network security, his narrow focus meant that he failed to notice when he crossed over an invisible line. With such a negative view of his customers, he failed to weigh the inconvenience he caused them against the benefits of slightly heightened network security. When queried about alternative ways of dealing with these issues, he admitted that in some cases he could have plugged this or that security hole in a more customer-friendly way, but he just didn't think of it.

The goal of the information commons is to make it possible for the academic community to use technology in the ways that are most productive and responsive to their needs. If their visits to the commons are unproductive because they are not allowed to do what they want to do, they will not return. Too often, the planners of technology facilities focus more on hardware and software than on customers. To provide a feast of wonderful resources and then make it impossible for those invited to the banquet to enjoy them almost amounts to cruelty. Yet this is how many information commons inadvertently treat their student users. Technicians, fearful of intruders, impose so many security restrictions that some of the most useful features and functions go unused.

With a well-informed, user-friendly technical staff, it is possible to maintain a secure system and still allow customers to adapt technology to their personal needs. For example, they will be more productive if they can move information between the library's desktop computers and their own laptops. Work groups are more efficient when they can easily make changes to a single document from several different computers, whether these happen to be personally owned laptops or library equipment. It has always seemed to me that there is a great divide between technical staff who focus on their customers and technical staff who focus entirely on machines. Those in the latter category may have only a vague idea of how and why those machines will be used.

As I write, I am thinking of one technician who caused no end of trouble to his library. He alternately expounded on the wonders of state-of-the-art equipment and the irritations he had to endure with stupid library users. The library director could never quite figure out why the technician thought the library should purchase the bleeding-edge technology he recommended when he obviously thought library users were incapable of using it. Even though this staff member possessed excellent technical skills, he was the wrong choice for the library. Though he wowed his supervisor with his expertise, he should never have been hired. When such people are involved in planning an information commons, they will fail to understand how hardware and software will be used by real people. They have spent so little time watching customers as they attempt to complete assignments or apply new technology to their projects that they miss the small details that can make a computer facility all but useless. For example, they configure a firewall in such a way that the people who need resources can't access them. They lock down PCs so completely that the student who finds the perfect journal article can't save it.

The Information Commons and the Academic Bureaucracy

Occasionally, a library planning group runs afoul of other campus departments that have jurisdiction over some aspect of technology. Groups may become so immersed in the details of their plan that they fail to realize that they do not live and work in isolation. The mention of firewalls in the last paragraph reminds me of a story of one particular commons that failed to anticipate the wrath of the department that controlled the campus network. Interdepartmental conflict is natural, and when one of the departments happens to have a large budget at its disposal, jealousy can result. In this case, the powerful department decided that the library had handled security issues so poorly that it was a threat to the entire university network. It took weeks before the library staff and customers regained full access to the network. Whether the library was actually at fault is hard to say, but it is doubtful that genuine security issues were at the heart of the conflict. Much of the wrath that fell on the heads of the library planners could undoubtedly have been avoided if they had been more politically astute. Library directors and other high-level library administrators are accustomed to this kind of interdepartmental strife, but staff members who rarely meet and compete with the administrative bureaucracy may not understand how inflated egos can sabotage the best of plans.

One effective strategy is to include members of other campus departments in the planning group. Although this can be an effective solution, the group may become too large and cumbersome. It might be more helpful to invite members of other departments to specific meetings where they are asked for their input. Outsiders who have little stake in the new facility may become bored and find better things to do with their time than attend meetings. I heard the tale of one campus computer administrator, for example, who never showed up for library meetings. Finally, the planning group was unable to meet a deadline because they lacked her input. They complained to the library director, who in turn contacted the administrator's boss. It turned out she had been using meeting times to run personal errands while complaining to her superior that her work for the library was taking up too much of her time.

STAFFING THE INFORMATION COMMONS

Because the information commons is a recent innovation, there is not yet a widely accepted model for staffing the area. It is agreed, of course, that more customer assistance is needed than in most other parts of the library. However, based on my visits to academic libraries, it appears that an efficient staffing plan has yet to be developed. Most commons provide a technician (or at least a technically sophisticated student worker) to assist computer users. A second staff member with some reference skills is usually available, and one or the other responds to all requests for help. Larger facilities, of course, assign more staff members to the commons, but I have not discovered how and why staff are usually chosen. Because these are uncharted seas, it seems as if staffing is largely trial and error. Perhaps a better way of identifying staffing needs is to begin with the customers who use the commons every day. Who are they and what are their needs? Let's begin with the needs that are the easiest to address and progress from there.

E-mail Users and Internet Surfers

Meeting the needs of these users is relatively easy. The basic applications they use are very simple and reliable, so student technicians can meet most of their needs. As long as the network is functioning properly and individual computers are communicating with the network, little additional help is needed. Student assistants, however, are not very good at explaining things. They may know how to do something, but they find it difficult to share their skill with others. Occasionally, for example, they encounter computer-phobic users, often older, nontraditional students going back to school after many years' absence. Student technicians may do little but confuse these customers. They may unconsciously communicate contempt for their ignorance and make them feel even more incompetent. Working with new computer users, especially those who have acquired a negative attitude toward technology, requires a knowledgeable staff member who is a natural teacher. In fact, you might say that initiating nervous newbies is almost an art form. What is needed is a staff member who possesses excellent teaching skills and genuine sympathy for these customers. In my experience, this describes many librarians I have known. Of course, a paraprofessional may possess these same skills, but, either way, this role of guide and teacher is an important one.

Subscription Database Users

Of all the customers we encounter in the information commons, this is the group we may feel most obligated to support. After all, they are using library resources, and so they are depending on us in much the same way they always have. The computer is merely a different medium. Because we feel so much affection for this group, do we give them the kind of support they need? My library visits indicate that we could certainly do better. It might be useful here to divide these "home team" users into two groups.

Inexperienced Searchers

The first group consists of inexperienced students who have not yet learned how to research a topic. We usually encounter these students as freshmen in our information literacy classes. A good old-fashioned reference interview would be tremendously helpful to them at this point. They must learn to articulate their questions, clothing them in the words that can be typed into a search engine. They also need to decide how these words relate to one another, so knowledge of basic Boolean operators is helpful. As we all know, these students are probably the ones least likely to set time aside for this purpose. Their moment of truth often comes when they find themselves sitting in front of a computer with no idea what they're going to do next. It takes an experienced reference librarian to seize these teaching moments. A few questions, a small dose of information judiciously administered, and the student returns to his project armed with new skills and insights. Extend the discussion too long and you'll lose the student's attention. Cut it short and both you and your customer have lost an important opportunity.

Experienced Searchers

The second group of customers who use our subscription databases has more sophisticated skills. Perhaps they are graduate students, or at least experienced undergrads. They may be successful Google searchers, but our databases pose unique challenges. Each vendor in the database market provides a somewhat different user interface. They are all much more user friendly than they once were, but they still differ from web-based search engines and from one another in many significant ways. As librarians, we know that it is possible to get much more out of databases than most users realize. Advanced searching, guided searching, and expert searching often produce different results in different databases. Understanding and making use of such distinctions can help pinpoint the information customers need and save them time spent poring over hundreds of useless citations. The skills needed may be somewhat technical, but they should never be left to technicians. If we think of a database as a vast library, these are the skills needed to find one's way among the multitude of resources. They are, therefore, reference skills. Mastering them is essential to satisfying sophisticated information needs.

Specialized Skills

I emphasize this point because again and again I have encountered commons staff—professional, paraprofessional, and technical—who didn't know how to search a database well enough to guide their customers. Perhaps because database producers, not librarians, designed these programs, librarians do not feel responsible for mastering them. Where once librarians somehow managed to learn those eccentric filing rules of the past and knew precisely which volume held what unexpected fact, some of their modern descendants seem unwilling to put any real effort into mastering the twists and turns of today's information highway.

If we are to provide high-quality customer service, we must make it possible for our customers to satisfy their information needs. Soon after I began my visits to academic libraries, I tried asking the commons staff for help with a somewhat difficult search. Mine were not trick questions, but they did require some knowledge of advanced search techniques. In general, the result was disappointing. Only occasionally was a staff member really helpful. More often, they referred me to a help screen or failed to suggest a feature that might have produced better results. It wasn't long before I gave up on testing staff members because I felt guilty—like a disloyal spy. By that point, however, I had formulated some thoughts about the staff members most and least likely to provide useful information. There was no question that librarians permanently assigned to the commons were the best. Whether they were called reference librarians or automation librarians or held some other designation, they were tops. Rarely did they fail to take my question seriously and give me at least one new tool to help fine-tune my search.

What was odd, however, was my discovery that other librarians were also the least helpful ones. These were the ones who were assigned to the commons for only a few hours a week. Even student workers were more competent because at least they had good computer skills. It was not that these librarians did not do their best. They bent over backward to help me, standing or sitting at my computer while they tried one bad idea after another. Finally, a paraprofessional might notice us and come to the rescue—almost never, however, with the insight displayed by the permanently assigned librarian.

Earlier in this book, I described the changes that have taken place in reference services in the last twenty years or so, especially the trend to staff the reference desk with librarians from other departments. The justification is that they can bring expertise from their own areas of specialization. The area where they're not fully competent is reference. I've become increasingly convinced that all librarians are not natural reference librarians, and real expertise is needed to be truly effective. The information commons also calls for specialized skills, and those skills take time to acquire. It is necessary that staff members develop specific skills directly related to this particular assignment; in other words, that they know what customers don't know. It is also necessary that staff members are able to communicate this information in a way that can be readily understood, and teaching skills do not come naturally to everyone.

TELEPORTING THE LIBRARY

Many academic librarians will remember the days when larger universities had a plethora of libraries. There might be a psychology library, a chemistry

library, and a political science library, as well as a religion library and a biology library. Even though these departmental libraries were usually sparsely
funded and poorly staffed, they were still extremely expensive. Resources
were unnecessarily duplicated, and each library had a tendency to become
a separate little kingdom, doing everything a little differently from the main
library. Professors with too much time on their hands created their own clas-
sification systems that supposedly made more sense in their disciplines than
Dewey or LC. In some cases, the multiple libraries created a bureaucratic
nightmare that was almost impossible to administer effectively. Departmental libraries were torn between allegiance to the library system and to their
academic departments. Power-hungry administrators sometimes counter-
manded library policies, and territorial battles were frequent.

The Closing of Departmental Libraries

When hard times came to academe, most of these libraries were gradually
closed, leaving only libraries in large and powerful professional schools like
medicine and law. Many library directors breathed a sigh of relief, since
they were no longer pulled in so many different directions and staff could
be more efficiently used. The problem was that academic departments were
far from happy. Students who had once spent hours studying in their departmental library did not necessarily find their way to the main library. The
staff member, whether professional or paraprofessional, who presided over
the departmental library's lone public service desk really understood what
students needed and how they used a library. Students developed friendly,
comfortable relationships with their "librarians" and were far more likely to
pour out their problems and ask for help. Because faculty members no longer stopped by the departmental library for coffee and a bit of gossip, they
were less likely to order books or get help with a journal article required for
tenure. They no longer had a personal librarian who understood their needs,
and they were less likely to seek out a stranger at the main library and invite
him or her to class when they were discussing research skills.

When library funding improved, the departmental libraries were not
reinstated. Instead, the central library was greatly enlarged, becoming a
huge barn or warehouselike building. Even with expensive furnishings and
thick carpet, the new libraries were not comfortable, friendly places. They
were not cozy places where students naturally encountered their friends and
classmates.

Embedded Librarians in the Virtual World

Let's look in on the librarians at Ball State University. They are part of an innovative trend in academic libraries that has created *embedded librarians*. The term is derived from the journalists who have been placed in military units to provide more accurate and gripping news reports. Embedded academic librarians, however, are more involved with the classroom than the battlefield. Ball State librarians use Blackboard to "embed" themselves in selected university classes. Librarians are able to view course outlines and assignments and to participate in online discussion groups. Because they possess an in-depth understanding of course content, they are able to provide more relevant and timely reference help. Because they are in a sense part of the class, they find many reasons to exchange e-mails with both students and faculty, often resulting in face-to-face consultations and other personalized services. Younger, less experienced students often have difficulty analyzing and communicating their research needs. When librarians are already familiar with course content, students' comfort levels rise rapidly.

Librarians at the University of Rhode Island provide support to their university's distance learning courses, which are offered online using the course management system WebCT. As with Blackboard, embedded librarians are able to participate in e-mail exchanges and discussion board postings. They can provide just the right amount of instruction as is appropriate for a particular assignment and provide it at exactly the right moment. Unlike traditional library instruction sessions, they are at hand when the time is ripe, when research topics are being chosen or when students encounter dead ends. In answering one student's reference question, they are often able to provide needed information to the entire class.

Embedded Librarians in the World of Bricks and Mortar

Let us return to our imaginary library and look in on some librarians inspired by the exciting tales of these embedded librarians. Working closely with the teaching faculty, they develop a program that eventually succeeds in embedding librarians in many online courses. Of course, this works best when faculty are able to work with the same librarian again and again, so librarians gradually develop closer relationships with academic departments. Let's imagine, however, that one academic department is not content with this arrangement. "We're here and you're there," they argue. "Virtual reference help is great, but what about our other classes? What about our face-to face students?" The librarian is struck by the logic of this argument. "If I can do my library work on the third floor of the library, why couldn't I do it on the second floor of the nursing building?"

The nursing faculty is delighted with the idea and finds a convenient nook for the librarian's workstation. Just as it was important to create a comfortable work environment on the third floor of the library, it's necessary that embedded librarians have equally comfortable spaces in classrooms or other buildings in order to meet their personal and professional needs. Embedded librarians are essentially creating tiny branch libraries, so some space is needed. Computer hardware and software are, of course, essential, especially a reliable printer and a high-speed Internet connection, because librarians will be working closely with main library staff members, students, and faculty on their research projects. This is the ideal spot for a small ready-reference collection, so a few bookcases should be included in the planning. As time goes by, the faculty will gradually realize that they can trust their embedded librarians with some of the treasures they hide in their office closets. These are the books and media programs that they keep on permanent loan from the library or purchase with departmental funds. Because they were always locked up, they were never available to the students and faculty who could have used them.

Staying Connected

As you can see, there will probably be a tendency to place more and more resources under the embedded librarian's umbrella. In itself, this doesn't create many problems, but occasionally conflicts erupt over "ownership" of the embedded librarian herself. There is ample evidence that such conflicts can greatly diminish the effectiveness of the program. It is essential that librarians working outside the library consider themselves wholly a part of the library and wholly a part of the academic department to which they are assigned. This may not add up mathematically, but it makes perfect sense when it comes to allegiances. When one or the other connection becomes too tenuous, programs become ineffective and may completely fall apart. It is therefore a good idea to split the librarian's work schedule between the library and the academic department. If the academic department is comfortable having its librarian attend faculty meetings, these serve as excellent opportunities for networking. Similarly, librarians should continue to attend librarians' meetings. This can obviously result in a lot of time spent in meetings, but it may be possible to relieve embedded librarians of other responsibilities that are less relevant to their work.

Because there are many opportunities for conflict and misunderstanding, it is essential that the basic conditions under which the arrangement functions are set out in writing. In general, embedded librarians are paid by the library. They are evaluated and considered for promotion by the library, with input from their academic departments. Reporting lines may be somewhat complicated, but it must be understood that this is an outreach program of the library and an extension of the library. In some situations, academic departments may formally share librarians with the library, paying half their salaries as well as supervising and evaluating them as if they were their own part-time staff members. There comes a point in this progression, however, when the librarian is no longer part of the library. When this happens, cooperation often ceases and competition takes over. What makes embedded librarian programs effective is their ability to serve as a bridge or a channel of communication through which resources and expertise travel back and forth. When territorial conflicts erupt and kingdom building takes over, bridges collapse and everyone involved suffers.

Creating Community

Many of the more successful embedded librarian programs, of course, operate from cyberspace. Librarians are virtually embedded in online courses, distance learning programs, and digital libraries. These programs have brought the library and its resources to a great many students who might otherwise be unable to find their way across the vast reaches of the information universe. When the embedded librarian comes face-to-face with students and faculty, the result can be even more exciting. When such librarians become attached to an academic program, they create hubs around which a strong sense of community can emerge. Most of the better-known projects have been developed on large university campuses where students may not even be acquainted with other members of their own programs. Wherever the embedded librarian is stationed, faculty and students tend to gather. Typically, the librarian is assigned an office space and, occasionally, a classroom becomes available. However, even a small space can accommodate a few computer workstations and a miniscule collection of print resources. As students and faculty drop by to request a book or search a database, they gradually come to feel connected with both the library and with the members of their own community.

Support for Embedded Librarians

Naturally, an important part of the service provided by the embedded librarian is making resources available that are housed in the main library. Typically, students and faculty make requests, either online or by personally bringing them to the embedded librarian. Materials are then pulled from the library's shelves and delivered to the academic department, where they await pickup. Carrying out this function efficiently requires considerable interaction with and support from the staff in the central library. Of course, it may be possible for embedded librarians to gather up materials during the hours when they are working at the central library, but it is certainly not cost-effective to devote a great deal of professional time to a clerical task. Instead, a robust support system must be in place to make the embedded librarian program successful. In other words, it is important that library staff members see the program as part of their responsibilities, whether or not they are serving as embedded librarians.

During the course of my interviews with librarians, I found considerable indifference and even hostility toward embedded librarian programs. One woman I interviewed told me that this was simply spoon-feeding students and faculty. The embedded librarian was doing their work and it wasn't fair to the rest of the library's customers. In other words, she was equating personalized service with spoon-feeding. I found myself ruminating over this interview for some time afterward. What was it that these library customers were getting that they weren't entitled to? Essentially, the answer was "good service." It seemed to me that the disgruntled librarian begrudged these customers the opportunity to be well served, to obtain library materials without wasting hours of their time. She seemed to think it was unfair that they could actually get to know their librarian and look on him as a friend and colleague. Of course, the faculty and students of this department were getting better service than the customers of the central library, and her response was to impose equality—in other words, less service for everyone.

I think what we are learning from embedded librarian projects is that the library can assume a central place in academic life when we come close enough to our customers, whether physically or virtually, to understand their needs. We all know the adage about walking in someone else's moccasins. Survey after survey has confirmed that librarians want to do just that; they really and truly care about their customers. They would be more than willing to see the world through the eyes of their customers if only they had sufficient opportunities. The university libraries that have been built and staffed during the past thirty years make this goal extremely difficult to achieve. Small, specialized libraries are not cost-effective, so we have watched universities' central libraries grow larger and larger. In a sense, we might say that each increase in size has corresponded with an expanding fissure separating individual librarians from their customers. The emergence of embedded librarians has given us the opportunity to recapture the personal relationships that characterized libraries of the past while, at the same time, offering the plethora of information resources that our present computer age can offer.

RESOURCES

Albanese, Andrew Richard. "Campus Library 2.0: The Information Commons Is a Scalable, One-Stop Shopping Experience for Students and Faculty." *Library Journal* 129, no. 7 (April 15, 2004): 30–33.

Beatty, Susan, and Peggy White. "Information Commons: Models for eLiteracy and the Integration of Learning," *Journal of eLiteracy* 2, no. 1 (2005): 10. Available at www.jelit.org/archive/00000052/01/JeLit_Paper_16.pdf.

Christensen, Clayton M., and Michael E. Raynor. *The Innovator's Solution: Creating and Sustaining Successful Growth.* Boston: Harvard Business School Press, 2003.

Crockett, Charlotte, Sarah McDaniel, and Melanie Remy. "Integrating Services in the Information Commons: Toward a Holistic Library and Computing Environment." *Library Administration and Management* 16, no. 4 (2002): 183.

Gjelten, Daniel R., Lisa Burke Marose, and Jeffrey A. Scherer. "The Architecture of an Idea: The Information Commons and the Future of the Academic Library." Paper presented at the EDUCAUSE Annual Conference, Denver, 2004. Available at www.educause.edu/ir/library/powerpoint/EDU04107.pps.

Keating, Shay, and Roger Gabb. "Putting Learning into the Learning Commons: A Literature Review." Postcompulsory Education Centre, Victoria University, Victoria, Australia, 2005, 11. Available at http://eprints.vu.edu.au/94/.

See the book's website for more resources on innovation: www.ala.org/editions/extras/woodward09768.

8

SHARING OUR VISION

Marketing the Academic Library

It's probably not an exaggeration to say that most of the people who work and attend classes on our academic campuses know very little about the library. They have a mental picture that may have been formed in high school or, in the case of faculty, long ago when they themselves were undergraduates. It will be difficult to convince them that the library you and the other members of the library staff have created is different from that mental image.

REACHING OUT TO THE ACADEMIC COMMUNITY

As we transform our libraries, we may even encounter opposition from both the teaching faculty and the college or university administration. Both groups may view the changes as unnecessary and wasteful. They may think they have a clear picture of what constitutes a "proper academic library." Students, on the other hand, may be almost completely unconscious of our existence. They may be aware that we can provide the books and journal articles on their course syllabi, but they don't really see how the library can fit into their lives. How are we to share our vision of the twenty-first-century library? How can we make students aware that the library could mean so much more to them than an assigned reading? How can we help faculty members focus on the future, not the past, and make them full participants in the transformation?

Let's begin with students. On the positive side, students have few preconceived ideas about what the library is and is not. Unless they had a particularly bad experience in high school, we will probably not have to battle stereotypes, as we do with faculty. On the negative side, however, students may walk past the library building every day but never enter its doors until they are juniors or seniors. In fact, surveys of college students often reveal that many have never visited the library. This means that the library faces much the same problem that retailers face when they seek to attract customers. Marketing strategies are needed to attract students, just as they are needed in many other areas of contemporary life. Nevertheless, the academic culture may hold such activities in contempt. Because librarians compare themselves with teaching faculty, they too may disdain the job of marketing their wares, comparing it to becoming used car salesmen.

One of the reasons why marketing may not be seen in a positive light is the way library staff members, especially librarians, have been taught to view their jobs. As we discussed in previous chapters, today's staffing patterns may exclude librarians from making decisions about their buildings and some services, de-emphasizing their nonacademic responsibilities. If they are not given a voice in such decisions, however, they may decide that these matters are beneath their dignity. They may consider attempts to make their buildings more customer friendly as unrelated to their own work and may daily walk past empty literature racks, inaccurate signs, and ugly carpet stains, believing that none of this is part of their job. They may also hear negative comments from students and fail to respond to the problems raised. In fact, they may even express agreement, implying that someone somewhere on high is not doing his or her job. Though academic librarians may actively seek to attract library customers, they may never make the connection between the library environment and library use.

FINDING THE TIME AND THE MONEY

Still another reason why the library staff may not put much effort into marketing is that there aren't funds available for this purpose. Academic librarians usually have far less control over their budgets than public librarians. Building-related expenses may be included in central, university-wide budget lines, and the library's own budget is often expended primarily on resources and personnel. If library directors were to add line items related to marketing, they might be opening themselves up to criticism. "Marketing! Why on earth should the library waste money on marketing when it can't provide this or that service?" Yet redirecting some funds, even if a relatively small sum of money, is essential for library transformation. Sharing our vision of what a library can and should be on the interpersonal level is the first step, but it is not enough. A practical plan for increasing community awareness of the library must be developed in concert with the custodial services department, faculty library committee, college or university administrators, and a host of other individuals and departments that are shareholders in the library's future.

Opening Communication

The difficulty we experience reaching out to our customers is, to some extent, the result of universally poor campuswide communication. To explain what I mean by this, it might be helpful to describe the one instance in my academic library career when faculty, staff, and students were clearly "in the know." And it was all because of a cook! I was working in a small college that had an extraordinarily good cafeteria that provided a delicious lunch buffet. Almost no one brought a bag lunch to campus; no one lunched at a restaurant, remained in his office, or went home to lunch. Instead, we all gathered in the cafeteria. This meant that everyone, including librarians, administrative staff, teaching faculty, and students, found themselves sitting with a different assortment of college community members every day. Typical conversation consisted of a lot of gossip and a lot of jokes. However, an enormous amount of useful information was exchanged. The food was so good (e.g., real homemade mashed potatoes) that even the president usually joined us. If a rumor was circulating around the college, questions would fly so fast and furiously that the poor president had difficulty eating his lunch.

As I say, this was the one and only time in my academic career that I actually felt I really knew what was going on. It has made me acutely aware that on most campuses, students, staff, and faculty live and work in separate realities. Each discipline is a small, isolated kingdom, and even faculty teaching in the same department may not find opportunities to communicate with one another. Because the library is neither fish nor fowl—neither an academic nor a fully administrative department—it may be even more isolated. In a typical business environment, most of the participants spend the same eight hours coming into repeated contact with one another. Faculty members may typically drive to campus for one or two morning classes, return home for the remainder of the day, and come back hours later to teach an evening class. They may go directly from parking lot to classroom without encountering anyone they know. Only if they have office hours during the day are they likely to see even members of their own departments, and verbal exchanges may be limited to greetings in the hallway. A full-time student may have a somewhat similar schedule, and part-time students come and go with hardly anyone being aware of their presence.

In such an environment, how can the library really become the center, the focal point, for the campus community? To answer this question, we must first ask how these potential customers communicate with one another. Only then can we discover how they can be made more aware of the library. So often, it seems to me that libraries have their own communication channels, and they imagine that those same channels are used by students and faculty. Too often the library is merely talking to itself.

The Library's Experience with Marketing

It is not as if marketing is new to academic libraries; we have long been producing publicity materials like newsletters and brochures. However, these are generally activities that take second or third place to more traditional academically focused library activities, especially as funding dwindles. Libraries rarely have a clear marketing plan. Instead, they do a little of this and a little of that. For example, they start a newsletter and then abandon it when staffing gets tight or some other project takes center stage. They produce a brochure or pathfinder with little attention to design principles and fail to notice when it becomes outdated. They accept the university webmaster's interpretation of the library, or that of a talented work study student who includes eye-catching Java scripting and a dozen spelling errors on the website. When he or she graduates, the website is relegated to the back burner, and it continues to advertise last year's programs. All this adds up to marketing gone awry.

THE MARKETING PLAN

Most academic librarians would probably say that their libraries put considerable effort into publicizing their activities. Often, however, it seems as if it hasn't proven a worthwhile expenditure of time. After the library staff have put a lot of work into publicizing an event or a service, customers continue to be either unaware of its existence or unwilling to take advantage of the opportunity. In other words, marketing has not proven useful in advancing the goals of the library. Naturally, such experiences tend to be discouraging and serve as an excuse for us to hide our light under a bushel.

   If we were to take on the role of detectives and investigate the reasons for these marketing failures, we might discover that the publicity did not reach the right people. In other words, the customers who might need the service or enjoy attending the event didn't hear about it. Maybe the library staff assumed that their customers got their information from the same sources they did. In other words, the information was marketed in the wrong places to the wrong people. There are a number of other reasons why publicity efforts fail, but they can usually be boiled down to a lack of research and planning. Publicity cannot be effective when it is done hit or miss by different staff members in different ways. It is a waste of time when there's no coordinated plan to target the right customers through the right media and provide them with the right information.

In addition, libraries may be trying to market the wrong services. While a business probably wishes to market all its merchandise, libraries provide a number of services that are essential but difficult to market (e.g., cataloging and processing). They also provide services that are not worth marketing because they don't really serve customers either directly or indirectly, services that perhaps have outlived their usefulness. For this reason, library marketers will do well to consider the services themselves as well as strategies to make them more widely known. While businesses sometimes use marketing to create a need that doesn't exist, libraries must be held to a higher standard. To market our services both ethically and successfully, we must know that our customers need those services. Before we query our customers about how best to advertise a service, we must ask them how the service fits into their lives. The traditional business marketing plan can and should be enhanced by adding this needs component.

Coordinating Our Efforts

Marketing is such a complex subject and involves so many aspects of the library's operation that it requires a very organized approach. Business organizations have developed the "marketing plan" to make sure that the entire organization is working together. Of course, their bottom line gives them an advantage. Because their bottom line is to sell merchandise, and marketing is essential to achieving this goal, the roles of the different departments fall into place more easily. Their bottom line also gives them a clearer picture of their customers and the response they want from them.

Effective library marketing is very different from the stereotypical image we have of Madison Avenue. There is really no way for a library to separate marketing from customer service. We can't attract more customers unless we meet their needs. We can't meet their needs unless they tell us what they are. It is only when we are actually publicizing needed resources and services that we will attract customers.

Who Are the Library's Customers?

One would think that academic libraries would have a clear picture of their community and be able to target their marketing much more easily than a public library. Theoretically, this is true. An academic library knows that its community consists of faculty, students, and administrative staff, but its image of these potential library customers may be inaccurate or outdated. For example, some academic departments may have grown in recent years, while others have shrunk. The number of part-time, nontraditional students may be much larger than librarians imagine. The library may be continuing to focus on programs that no longer attract large numbers of students. Finally, student interests are very different from what they were ten or twenty years ago, and so the way they use the library may have changed as well.

You might be considering a new service that seems useful and that ought to be popular. Stop for a moment to imagine the customers who would be using the service. Would they be grad students, undergrads, or both? Would some disciplines be more likely to use the service than others? Which ones? The next step is to get a small group of customers together. Faculty input is useful, but I suggest your group be composed mainly of students for a more practical perspective. When I asked whether a particular service would be helpful, every focus group I've ever facilitated has said "yes" no matter what the nature of the service. It just sounded like a good idea to them. However, the library does not have the resources to implement each and every good idea. You'll want to know the circumstances under which these students would actually use the service. What kind of project might they be working on? How would it fit into their schedule? If there is significant turnaround time, would they really be willing to wait? If the service is related to leisure activities like a popular fiction collection, would they actually have time to use it? How long do they stick around campus?

Quite often, it seems that we have an inaccurate picture of our customers. Perhaps we were given certain types of assignments when we were in college. Unconsciously, we are thinking about our own long-ago needs and those of our classmates. Perhaps we have a pretty good idea of the needs of one discipline because we have a friend who teaches in that department. We may incorrectly assume that those needs are typical of many disciplines. The only way to find out if this is true or not is to ask. There's no substitute for querying real students and real faculty. If you don't know how to reach them, then you're not going to be able to market the new service to them either. Developing a practical strategy to identify and communicate with your customers must be at the center of any effective marketing plan.

The Mission Statement

If tomorrow you were to hold a brainstorming session, your very creative library staff could come up with dozens of ways the library could become more visible and more responsive to the academic community. However, they'd also come up with a lot of ideas that would not be worth pursuing. The expenditure in time and effort would detract from other more important projects, and the results would not be worth the investment. How will you know which ideas fit into which category? There's no easy answer, and libraries frequently become sidetracked with less productive projects. However, the library's mission statement can provide a reasonably direct road map for getting you to your destination.

As we've mentioned, a business organization's focus is on its bottom line. In other words, for a business to be successful, it must make money. Nearly all its activities are either directly or indirectly focused on this goal. Having one clear goal simplifies planning and tends to keep everyone in the organization moving in the same direction. Academic libraries have a hard time focusing their attention on a single goal, and staff members may actually be moving in different and contradictory directions. If we look at our library's mission statement, however, we will probably find that we have the seed for a bottom line. That's why it is worth putting the time into a mission statement that really has some "oomph" to it. If your library's mission statement is similar to those of most libraries, you have already identified academic community participation in the library as your goal and, therefore, the library equivalent of the bottom line. Of course, the mission statement is usually brief, characterized by boilerplate language, and it's philosophical in tone rather than practical. It is possible to defend a wide variety of different and possibly conflicting plans by citing its stirring phrases. Nevertheless, this is a place where you can begin.

Unfortunately, this vague concept of public involvement does not provide the same degree of direction as a monetary goal. What kind of participation are you envisioning, and how will you prioritize different types? For example, it might be possible to bring people into the library to attend sociology classes or eat lunch or attend an athletic study hall. Is this what you mean by participation? You will need to clothe your goal in words that are specific and precise enough to evaluate the role such activities might play.

Some academic libraries have created a mission statement as an obligatory exercise. The staff may simply have been going through the motions, and your library's mission statement may contain nothing but platitudes and plagiarized verbiage from other libraries. That is not going to provide the kind of guidance you'll need, not only to develop your marketing plan but to make a wide variety of different decisions that will determine your library's future. If your library does not have a mission statement or it is so vague that it does not at least suggest a library bottom line, now is the time to write or rewrite one that really meets your needs.

Identify Customer Needs

Once the mission statement is in place, you will want to do some extensive research on the needs of your community. Let's assume that you have devoted some time and effort to identifying your community in some detail, and you have improved communication sufficiently that you can query students and faculty directly. Many of the needs they articulate cannot really be met by the library, but it's surprising how many of them can be reworded as a need for information. As librarians we are accustomed to measuring what we do, in other words, how many books we circulate, how many classes we teach, how many customers use the Internet. For our needs assessment, we must look honestly at what we are not doing. It is helpful to conduct surveys and use other data-gathering techniques. However, we must distinguish between those aimed at library users and those intended to reach the broader academic community. Of course, we want to serve our regular customers better, but our marketing effort should be focused on people who do not fall into this category.

Focus Groups

A few paragraphs ago, I mentioned using focus groups to get to know your customers. Focus groups, as you probably know, are a qualitative research method that involves asking a group of people about their attitudes toward a product or service. Marketing firms often use focus groups to find out about consumer preferences. They want to know how people will react to different names for a new automobile model or to an advertising slogan. Questions are asked in a group setting, and the participants talk freely with one another and with the group facilitator. Because this is a form of qualitative rather than quantitative research, the results can't be interpreted numerically and so are not precise. Nevertheless, it has been found that focus group validity can be quite high. Unlike quantitative studies, they can generate new ideas and information. The discussion may go in an unexpected direction, and an idea voiced by one participant sparks a more interesting one from another participant, providing a completely new and unexpected perspective.

In general, focus groups are a good way to begin painting a portrait of your customers. I've found, however, that discussing the library may be a little like talking about religion or motherhood. It's a kind of sacred cow that polite young people (and middle-aged ones too) may not want to criticize; they don't want to hurt your feelings. It can be difficult to get people to say what they really think. Seek out someone in your university who has worked with focus groups—perhaps a member of the business faculty. Find out if he or she would be willing to facilitate library focus groups or, even better, train library staff members in focus group techniques.

Interviews

Interviews can also reap a lot of useful information, but they must be carefully structured to be really productive. We all know that people like to talk about themselves, and that may actually be the reason they agree to be interviewed. Some of the things they want to tell us are helpful and some aren't. We need to keep our interview subjects on topic, sharing information that can actually be useful in developing and fine-tuning library services. Again, search your university for a marketing professional. Although we librarians are especially good at finding answers in books and periodicals, the experience of someone who has extensive professional experience in marketing can be even more useful.

Whether we are gathering information from individuals or from groups, we must distinguish between insiders and outsiders. The opinions of regular library users are useful to us because they already have opinions about the library based on their personal experience. Outsiders are members of the academic community who do not use our services, and they represent the majority of students and faculty. If the library is to reach out to them, it will have to look into their lives and discover where it can fit into their work, study, leisure, and personal routines. Unfortunately, we tend to expend much of our marketing effort trying to make these customers conform to our plans rather than fitting into theirs.

Surveys and Questionnaires

Quantitative research is typically conducted with surveys or questionnaires. The questions created for these instruments can give us some idea of whether problems and concerns that come out in interviews and focus groups are widespread or are unique to particular customers. In other words, an interview or focus group can tell us that at least one student has experienced a particular problem. What it can't tell us is whether the problem or experience is common to a large segment of the student body. Devising a questionnaire to sample the academic community allows us to estimate the prevalence of the problem.

Establishing the validity of a questionnaire can be an exhaustive process, so it's important to know whether statistically demonstrated validity is important to your planning process. The more important the decision, the more necessary it is to put time and expertise into developing a valid survey instrument. However, one innovative library I visited was very effective in communicating with its customers, and it rarely worried about statistical significance. This library had an information desk located quite near the entrance; traffic patterns brought customers within just a few feet of the desk no matter whether they were entering or leaving the library. When the library staff was considering a new program, they frequently created a brief, "quick and dirty" questionnaire that was distributed and collected at the information desk. No attempt was made to establish validity. These brief questionnaires were simply a way of establishing an informal channel of communication with library customers, and they were extremely effective. More formal instruments were used to survey noncustomers; these informal ones functioned more like thermometer or barometer readings.

Another library spent about eighteen months developing, validating, administering, and interpreting a survey. The work was extremely well done, and an article in a highly respected library journal came out of it. However, several months into the survey project, some year-end funding became available. This might have made it possible to implement the plan that was under consideration, but that would have meant implementing it without statistical validation. The planning group chose to forgo the funding and continue with the survey. Years have now passed, the survey results were very positive, but the project has been placed on the back burner. Funding is no longer available, and the librarians have turned their attention to more pressing matters. This is a hard call for librarians. Good data are extremely important, but it may be that libraries don't really have the resources to seek perfection. Perhaps a compromise would have produced better results, a compromise somewhere between "highly professional" and "quick and dirty." As long as we understand the limitations of our survey instruments, we can often obtain some very useful information from them.

Interpreting the Data

The value of customer-focused research, whether qualitative or quantitative, formal or informal, from surveys, focus groups, or interviews, is that it enables you to learn what your customers want and need. It also provides opportunities to discover how best to communicate with them. Deciding how you will respond to this information is at the heart of your marketing plan. Which of the library's services only require better communication with customers to be successful? Which services cannot be successful, no matter how much publicity they receive? Which services does the research indicate are missing altogether? It is only when you have matched library services to customer needs that it's time to ask the question: how will you spread the word?

To answer this question, you will need to know about the obstacles that stand in your way, the barriers that will make communication between the library and its customers difficult. You'll probably discover that there are many. There is little point in identifying marketing goals if you don't really understand why the library has failed to achieve similar goals in the past. Most library staffs have always been interested in making their customers happy. They have always engaged in some form of marketing, even if it was not in an organized way. Could it be possible that, once again, they have been planning in terms of what they think customers should want rather than their expressed needs? Even the best focus groups and interviews will not result in change if, deep down, library staff members believe that they know best.

Reaching Customers

Another essential part of your research is discovering the ways in which your customers get their information. You might do well to begin by assuming that your customers do not use the same communication channels as the library staff. For example, the library's website is a very important source of information about library resources, services, and events. It is one of the few information conduits that the library can fully control, but only the library's regular users see it. If you usually communicate with your customers through your website and in-house publications, then you're probably preaching to the choir. As you survey customers, find out what they read and where they go when they're online. Do they read the student newspaper? Where do they hang out on campus? Does your city have any tabloid-size publications that cover the local music scene? Check out the literature racks on campus and ask students which publications they tend to pick up. Does the library need a presence on MySpace or Facebook? Ask your customers.

Put It in Writing

A marketing plan should be a written document, but I am always a little suspicious of written plans. I have had all too many negative experiences with strategic plans that had no impact on either the university or the library's development. It is too often the fate of formal plans to be filed away and forgotten. Nevertheless, the high degree of coordination needed to pull together different library departments and constituencies makes it necessary to have a common reference. Include in the plan a regular schedule of meetings to review progress, and don't type the last period or press the print button until you have set approximate dates.

Although you will probably want to read some marketing plans before you set your own to paper, resist the temptation to copy from them. You tend to begin by rationalizing that there's no point in wasting your time over boilerplate language. You'll be using your own time and that of other team members more efficiently if you concentrate on the "meat" of the plan. Unfortunately, you tend to find more and more impressive lines from other marketing plans that can easily be integrated into your own plan, and the so-called meat shrinks accordingly. However, your team's eyes will grow glassy as they look over your boring verbiage. Before you know it, you've produced a marketing plan that no one's actually read or is really committed to. Occasionally, a library hires a consultant to write a marketing plan. The result may be a document that is virtually identical to the one written for his or her last client. Though the final document may appear less impressive, perhaps it would be better to do without boilerplate language entirely.

Primary and Secondary Markets

At this point, it's a good idea to review your progress. Remember that you began the process of developing a marketing plan by focusing on your mission statement. Don't forget to revisit it often. It will serve as your road map and will help you avoid spinning your wheels or concentrating your efforts on less productive projects. As a second step, you defined your market. Who are your primary customers? Don't forget to consider other people who have come to depend on your services. Students and faculty represent your primary market. The local community is of secondary importance in your planning. What about the gray areas? Your library supports staff development, as well as a variety of town/gown cooperative projects, faculty recreational interests, and community priorities. How supportive can you be of these diverse needs? How do they compare with service to students? These functions are not equally important, and it's important to confront such questions. Marketing efforts should not raise unrealistic expectations.

Fine-Tuning Goals and Planning for Results

Now that you know more about your customers, as well as the relative importance of reaching other constituencies, you should consider what broad results you want to achieve. Let's say that your broad marketing goal is an increase in library usage. Even better, you might begin immediately to think in concrete terms and specify that the result will be a 10 percent increase in library usage. How long will it take to achieve this goal? How might you achieve it? Break this broad goal up into component parts that are easier to work with. You might, for instance, establish categories like reserve circulation, information literacy classes, or head count, setting subgoals for each one. Then work with the library staff to further define your expectations. What has to be done and when must it be done? What interim objectives will ultimately contribute to attaining the larger goal? Does one depend on another?

The library lacks both the money and the staffing to carry out the kind of marketing campaign that a large corporation might envision. The secret of success lies in the creative use of the resources you do have at your disposal. Consider what other resources might be available to the library and how you might use them wisely. Colleges and universities are fortunate to be able to call upon an extraordinary number of experts in different fields. Take advantage of your community, especially in areas where librarians traditionally have little experience. Does your college or university have a marketing or public relations department? Visit with the director and ask about the services available. Would he or she be willing to do a workshop for the library staff? Marketing faculty often need class projects and may be delighted to work with the library. Similarly, commercial design classes may be able to provide professional-looking materials at little or no cost. Discard elaborate plans that will interfere with the library's efficient operation, but remember that the marketing effort is also essential to the library's well-being.

Looking at the Big Picture

Where does the library fit into the academic community? What is its role in this external environment? There are probably some elements in that environment that are actually hostile to the library and others that, though not hostile, effectively interfere with the library's freedom to move forward. What are they? From where do these challenges originate? Of course, we create many of our own problems, but not all of them by any means. Consider the attitude of the college or university administration. How do they feel about the library? Do they understand its importance? Are there individuals or possibly administrative departments that seem to have a particularly negative attitude toward the library, which impacts the achievement of library goals? Are there departments that view the library as encroaching on their territory?

Are there changes on the horizon that will ultimately impact the library? For example, a new president can precipitate a major reorganization. How is this likely to help or hurt the library? Are some elements within the power structure of the institution gaining or losing power? What political shifts are becoming apparent?

Once you have a clear picture of the library's environment, consider the future. Where do you see the library in five years? Ten years? How might the challenges you've identified in the environment affect the library? Consider best- and worst-case scenarios. Then think about how the library's own strengths and weaknesses fit into these scenarios. How can the library maximize its strengths? How might it be possible to either eliminate weaknesses or minimize their importance by pointing the library in other directions?

Market Segments

It's a good idea, once you have this clear picture of your environment, to subdivide it into what the business world calls market segments. Students, of course, have different library needs from faculty, and beginning students need different services than graduate students working on their dissertations. To bring each group into the library, a somewhat different approach will be needed. Of course, many customers fit into more than one group. For example, many staff members take advantage of their tuition remission benefits to complete their undergraduate education or work on graduate degrees. They also have recreational and professional needs that send them in different directions. Just be sure your information is accurate and you are not working with a picture of the academic community as it was ten or twenty years ago.

Next, consider primary markets that you are not reaching. Which are the groups in the academic community that are not making use of the library? If you haven't already done so, design ways to sample the library's users, and compare the results with what you know about the college or university as a whole. Are library users typical of the general student population? Do you see roughly the same racial, ethnic, age, and gender ratios? Adapt your strategies to focus some of the library's marketing efforts on underserved customers. What new services might attract these groups? How can the library reach them more effectively?

How is your library perceived by the academic community? Which of your customers are most satisfied with the services you provide? What about the ones who do not use your services? This is where the results of those focus groups, surveys, and interviews are important. There is no point in redesigning services and publicizing these changes to the community if customers don't want or need them. What is it that makes the library unique? What does the library have to offer that other campus facilities lack? For example, what does the library information commons have that campus computer labs don't?

The Marketing Budget

Never forget that each of your plans comes with a price tag. What do you estimate to be your direct and indirect expenses? Don't forget to include personnel costs in your budget; when staff are occupied with marketing activities, they may not be getting other jobs done. For example, it may be necessary to hire temporary staff or outsource some functions. The library's usual one-year budget cycle may not be enough time to achieve major marketing goals. Consider working with a twelve-month planning phase and a twelve-month implementation phase. If you are thinking in terms of making major changes in the library, you will need to plan for at least this period of time. You may even want to think in terms of a five-year plan. Then decide what you will do if funds are not forthcoming.

Remember that when you're planning even two years ahead, a lot of unexpected things can happen, and budget crises are frequent in academic libraries. If your library experiences an unexpected budget cut, how will it impact the marketing effort? In other words, what is your fallback position? How can you move forward without the funding you anticipated? The reason for dealing with this now is that a budget cut can throw the library into a tailspin. The anger and anxiety generated can cause staff to view all projects as impossible or doomed. Yet the need for a marketing program is never so critical as during a budget crisis.

The Time Line

Once you have a clear picture of how much time the entire project will require, you're ready to develop a time line. If you're thinking in terms of the two-year plan mentioned above, break the plan up into a series of interim steps. Which ones depend on other goals being achieved first? Remember that, in a sense, you will be planning to plan. The marketing plan is merely a road map, and it is important to have a clear, objective way of making sure that projects are on track. Consider how much time will be required to advance to each step or rung on the ladder and then set a date for each. Can you reasonably expect to achieve the end result twenty-four months from the starting date? If not, you may need to rework your budget, your goals, or your time line. I find it difficult, however, to plan more than two years ahead. So many new issues will emerge; so many participants will come and go. If you find yourself with a plan that seems to go on indefinitely, it may be worth rethinking the plan to fit it into a two-year time frame.

After the excitement of the initial planning stage dies down and enthusiasm begins to wane, little things will begin to bog you down. The staff begin saying to one another, "No, we can't do that now because this or that has come up. We'll get back to marketing next week or next month." Eventually, of course, the marketing plan is forgotten. Deadlines are, therefore, important. The first time the library misses a deadline, it should be viewed as a crisis demanding attention. Often it's the failure to reach a decision that holds up a project, so determine when each decision must be made.

Success or Failure?

How will you measure the success of the marketing effort? This must be decided in advance because we have a naughty habit of cheating. In other words, we want to feel successful, and so we pat ourselves on the back for achievements that have little to do with our initial intention. At the beginning of the project, it is essential to establish a clear, agreed upon outcome. Then at the end of the period, measure your achievements against it. Decide in advance just how success will be measured because, again, there is always that tendency to try to justify your efforts even if they were largely unsuccessful.

Don't forget that one goal of your marketing campaign should be reaching members of the academic community who may never set foot in the library. Our emphasis has been on bringing new faces into the library and better serving the needs of both old and new customers. However, we're also aware that there will be people who, despite our best efforts, may never use the library personally. Some of these noncustomers, especially upper-level administrators, are essential to the library's success. The library must find ways to bring its message to these decision makers. Although some may be regular library customers, you can't count on it. A special effort must be made to reach these community segments because they wield so much power over the library. Thus, a significant part of the plan should be focused on reaching them. How will you convince the dean or president that the library is worthy of more generous funding? How can the role of librarians be viewed more positively? The real decision makers may never enter the doors of the library, so other methods of reaching them will need to be devised.

Think of them as a special market segment that will require highly innovative techniques. Nevertheless, don't let a focus on the power structure cause you to ignore the needs of students who may be weak in power. Annual reports and funding requests are the ways libraries most often communicate with decision makers, and both can be used more effectively in the marketing effort. However, your marketing plan should also include new avenues of communication. Is it possible to meet with your decision makers more often? Might some of them occasionally attend library meetings? Be sure that they are on your distribution lists for library newsletters, brochures, and other publications. Let them know what the library is doing to reach faculty and students. Be sure the library's name is everywhere on campus. Don't forget that decision makers have their own information needs, although they might not realize how useful the library might be in meeting them. Consider a two-pronged approach. Provide a service that decision makers find useful, and then make them aware of the wide variety of library services that are available to the community as a whole.

Production of Promotional Materials

Promotional materials pose a special challenge because they always require more time than you initially imagine. When they're not ready in time to support other marketing activities, the result can be devastating. For example, the new website must be up and running before classes begin in the fall; the brochure must be ready in time to be distributed at the new student orientation; the newsletter must go out in time to advertise the upcoming program. Consider how the marketing time line is impacted by academic community events. How will you use each as an occasion to get out the library's message?

Design and Content Go Together

Speaking of promotional materials, good design costs no more than bad, but no matter how talented the staff, they cannot produce quality materials if they must borrow bits of time from their regular duties. Time must be blocked out when they can concentrate on a project and get it done. Marketing is not an extra; it is a necessity. Like everything else that is important to the library, it requires time, talent, and ongoing commitment. Central to any library marketing effort is desktop publishing savvy. Whether it's an annual report, a flyer advertising an upcoming library event, or even a lowly bookmark, most of the printed materials we produce require a basic knowledge of desktop publishing. A few years ago, the library was in good company when it distributed mimeographed newsletters and produced hand-lettered announcements. Before the arrival of personal computers, all but the larger businesses did the same. Most local stores did not have the money to hire professionals to design their publications, and local copy shacks had not yet made their appearance.

Today, many libraries continue to produce essentially the same kind of materials, but they are no longer in good company. Sophisticated word processors with desktop publishing features, as well as specialized programs like InDesign and QuarkXPress, have made it possible for almost anyone to create professional-looking promotional materials. Patrons accustomed to reading graphically sophisticated reports and responding to eye-catching fund-raising materials may take one look at the library's boring attempts and toss them aside. Here are some examples of publications that your library may be currently producing or that could make the library more visible to the community:

New book and media lists
Advertisements
Brochures
Fliers
Handbooks
Letterhead stationery
Newsletters
Pathfinders, bibliographies, and reading lists
Posters
Presentations (e.g., PowerPoint presentations)
Proposals
Reports
Signs

You might ask why it's worth putting staff time into desktop publishing. For example, why should you consider desktop publishing when you are writing a report? Isn't the main thing just to get the darn thing done, send it to the dean, and then forget about it? Definitely not; reports are opportunities to brag about your library's accomplishments. Potentially, they can serve as an excellent marketing tool, but not if no one wants to read them. Share your reports with other academic and administrative departments, being careful to make them really interesting. The same can be done with the library's strategic plan. Share it with your academic community. Allow them to be full participants in the library's hopes and dreams. How many people have read your library's mission statement? Nothing sells the library better than a brief or abbreviated mission statement printed on stationery, in the brochure that lists your hours and services, on flyers, and in newsletters.

Your attention to design principles can help focus the reader's attention on the library's accomplishments. Design can make important information stand out and catch the eye of the reader. It's no longer difficult to use tables and charts to present statistics in a way that makes it easy for the reader to understand what's really happening. Effective use of color can also keep readers interested. Good design focuses their attention on the positive achievements you want to emphasize. You might even consider condensing the report into a brochure and making it available to customers who would be reluctant to read a long, official-sounding report. Whatever you do, don't hide your light under a bushel. You and the library staff have been serving the community in interesting and rewarding ways; you have been developing new services and reaching new customers. This is your opportunity to make sure the community knows what you've been up to.

Attracting Attention

Since the advent of desktop computers, it seems as if everyone has been sending out snazzy-looking newsletters and other publications. You may be wondering how the library can compete with such professional-looking productions. In fact, you may feel that the library simply can't compete. Maybe you think that there's far too much work to be done to divert staff energies to anything as nonessential as impressive-looking marketing materials. Unfortunately, the truth is that you're already in competition. Your library is competing for the attention of people who have become accustomed to well-designed materials that are arriving daily in their mailboxes, eye-catching magazines, and elegant business correspondence. If your library's publications look amateurish and unprofessional, that may well contribute to customers' impression of the library itself.

The Publicity Machine

How else can we attract the attention of those people who are not yet our customers? Like any organization, we must advertise. The problem, of course, is that we have no advertising budget, or a very small one at best. Although librarians can be almost as effective marketers as corporate professionals, the job is extremely time-consuming. If you are contemplating a major effort to raise campus awareness of the library, it will be well worth the time, but you may feel that the library simply doesn't have time to spare.

The answer may be to create what, for lack of a better term, I will call a "publicity machine."

Let's say the library is sponsoring a workshop. How do you get out the word? You want a good turnout, but you and the staff have little time to devote to publicity. The answer is that you put your publicity machine into high gear. I use the word *machine* to emphasize the need for procedures that become almost automatic. You use the same well-developed procedures each time you need publicity, and each time they get smoother and speedier. For example, you have a to-do checklist, together with specific information about campus media. Your publicity machine streamlines the process. A template on your computer allows you to produce a news release for the student newspaper. A basic flyer template can be adapted easily for campus bulletin boards and faculty mailboxes in just a few minutes. If your institution has a radio or television station, the same information, slightly modified, can be sent to them as well. Just a few changes and the press release is ready for the local newspaper, and don't forget the library's home page, the campus calendar, and other web pages that spread the news.

When you're creating your publicity machine, consider how else you can get the word out. E-mail is perhaps the quickest and most efficient way to get information to a large number of people, so accurate, up-to-date e-mail addresses must be at your fingertips. Is there a new editor of the student newspaper? The old e-mail address may deliver your carefully written press release to a student who is no longer actively involved with the paper. E-mail your regular library users and ask them to print out your flyers and post them in their departments.

Printed flyers will need to be distributed immediately. A ready-to-roll plan that includes a list of designated staff and student workers who will distribute them at specified locations makes the process easier and much more dependable. Can you include an article in the faculty-staff newsletter? When is their deadline? All this information should be codified and stored in one place.

Newspaper and Newsletter Columns

For many libraries, a weekly or monthly newspaper or newsletter column is a wonderful way of revving up interest in the academic community. Your campus news organs may be delighted to publish a library column as long as the library understands their needs. Have you ever written a newspaper column before? It's really not very difficult. In fact, there's a tried-and-true formula that will help you construct a pretty good column with a minimum of effort. Begin with a personal detail. Ask the staff for stories about students and faculty who have said funny or touching things. The point is that readers are attracted by "people" stories. We always enjoy little personal details that make other people seem more human. Once you have a good opening paragraph, lead into a message about the library, letting readers know about new services and resources, or even existing ones that they may not be aware of. Using humor effectively is a good way to keep your readers with you. As a profession, we still must cope with the stereotype of the boring library and librarian. You will want to convey the feeling that the library is a delightful place to be and you and the staff are utterly fascinating people.

Sometimes it can be frustrating trying to think up a theme or topic for an article on deadline. Don't wait until the last minute. As you're talking with staff and customers, keep an ear out for a new angle, a different view of the library. If you should ever run out of ideas, you have thousands of them sitting on your shelves. When you've had a dull week, a quick overview of some newly arrived books or media programs is always appreciated. Keep your audience in mind. Remember that they don't look at things in quite the same way you do. For example, in April or May a student will probably be more interested in a book about summer jobs than a literary novel.

Readers will give you just a few minutes to tell them about the library. Then they'll be moving on to the exciting basketball game or the latest student grievance. What you write must relate to them personally. It must in some way speak to their lifestyles and interests. That means your first goal is to entertain, then inform. If you're in doubt about the best approach, read some columnists who write for your local newspaper. Which ones do you enjoy? Take a more in-depth look at those columns and try to discover precisely what it is that gets and keeps your attention.

Marketing Equals Communicating

Many, many books have been written on the fine points of marketing, and many are well worth reading. Some techniques work better for certain types of organizations, and the more you read, the more skilled you will become at choosing the best strategies for your particular needs. Never lose sight, however, of your own customers. You are offering a product that can truly improve the quality of their lives; you are offering resources and services that are valuable and well worth their time. You and the rest of the library staff believe in the library, and you have good reason to believe that your customers need what you have to offer. Whatever your marketing plan, whichever marketing stratagems you choose, be sure that your enthusiasm and your heartfelt zeal shine through. And remember that the library staff, in the end, can be your very best advertisement.

RESOURCES

Duke, L. M., et al. "How to Develop a Marketing Plan for an Academic Library." *Technical Services Quarterly* 25, no. 1 (2007): 51–68.

Hallmark, E. K., et al. "Developing a Long-Range and Outreach Plan for Your Academic Library: The Need for a Marketing Outreach Plan." *College and Research Libraries News* 68, no. 2 (February 2007): 92–95.

Koontz, Christie. "Customer-Based Marketing: Retail Interior Layout for Libraries." *Marketing Library Services* 19, no. 1 (January/February 2005). Available at www.infotoday.com/mls/jan05/koontz.shtml.

———. "Stores and Libraries: Both Serve Customers!" *Marketing Library Services* 16, no. 1 (January/February 2002). Available at www.infotoday.com/mls/jan02/koontz.htm.

Motin, S. "Reach Out to Your Community through Exhibits: Employing ALA Partner Grants as Part of Your Academic Library's Marketing Effort." *College and Research Libraries News* 68, no. 5 (May 2007): 310–13. Available at www.ala.org/ala/acrl/acrlpubs/crlnews/backissues2007/may07/exhibits.cfm.

9

CUSTOMER SERVICE

Making It All Come Together

As you've undoubtedly discovered by now, I am convinced that the survival of the twenty-first-century academic library depends on people, library people. The strides that we've made in expanding library resources and services into the virtual world are truly remarkable. Placing such a vast quantity of authoritative information at the fingertips of scholars is an accomplishment of which we can justly be proud. At the same time, I believe that if we let library buildings and face-to-face library services dwindle and die, we will be doing a great disservice to the academic world. Central to almost every library survival strategy is the library staff. It is only through their expertise and their interaction with customers that academic libraries can grow and prosper in the twenty-first century. Unfortunately, our customers are seeing less and less of reference librarians, permanent circulation staff, and many others whose primary responsibility was once public service.

While gathering information for this book, I visited the libraries of a large number of academic institutions, ranging from small community colleges to some truly mammoth universities. Based on those visits, I have reached some conclusions that to me are a major cause for concern. In the previous chapters, you accompanied me on tours of imaginary and not-so-imaginary libraries. As we visited different areas, it was not uncommon to find large areas of the library empty of permanent library staff members. Yes, we knew there were many people working behind the scenes to make the library function efficiently, but they were not part of most customers' experience.

THE CIRCULATION DESK

When we visited circulation areas, we discovered that most (perhaps eight out of ten) visible circulation staff members were students. This is not to say that we actually encountered eight or ten individuals, because the number was more likely to be two or three, supplemented by some self-checkout machines. Yet the library staff directory revealed that a substantial number of permanent library staff members were assigned to the department.

Interviews with circulation staff members revealed that the circulation staff, like most others with public service assignments, are of two minds about customer service.

On the one hand, staff members assert that they are dedicated to serving the needs of students and faculty. They consider customer service an important priority and worry about declines in circulation and library use. On the other hand, staff members feel that making themselves available at the circulation desk keeps them from getting their work done. There are necessarily busy times and slow times at all service desks, and during slow times staff feel that they are wasting their time. Their desks, they say, are piled with work. As one circulation staff member explained it, "Tiffany [a student worker] knows that I'm here if she needs me. I have to get my work done, but all she has to do is call. I'm happy to interrupt my work to serve the public."

Because this comment so perfectly encapsulated the attitudes I encountered, I wrote it down word for word. As is clearly apparent, the staff member makes a distinction between being available at the "front desk" and real work, which takes place behind the scenes at a very different desk. Twice she refers to her work as being something different from assisting customers. This was a library in which I was able to spend quite a bit of time, so I was able to cavesdrop on Tiffany and other student workers while they were attempting to assist customers. In general, the students were polite, but their responses to questions were not those of trained library staff members.

Defining Good Customer Service

What do I mean by the responses of a trained staff member? I had to answer that question for myself, and, of course, it was a difficult one. The physical layout of the library and the job descriptions of the circulation staff differ from library to library. In the end, I decided that a trained staff member would always be expected to provide enough information to satisfy a student or faculty member's immediate need or give clear directions to locate a librarian or other staff member who could do so. In addition, the trained staff member knows when student questions are not really the right ones, in other words, when students don't know what questions to ask. Novice library users are often so inexperienced or confused that some probing is needed to get at the underlying information need. Of course, reference librarians have developed the reference interview into an art form, but I've found that other permanent staff members are often very perceptive as well. They have worked with so many students that their mind-reading skills are well honed.

Having formulated this definition, I discovered that student staff members were at their best when looking up information on a computer. Questions like "How many books do I have out?" were usually answered correctly, although the student workers sometimes failed to bring up the right screens. When this occurred, they asked one another for help. In fact, they were many times more likely to seek help from another student worker than to go back into the workroom and "interrupt" the staff member I had spoken with. When questions concerned anything but circulation functions, student workers usually told customers to ask the reference librarian. Sometimes customers were told to go to "Reference," with no explanation of what "Reference" might be.

A high percentage of the questions were directional in nature and should not have required the help of a reference librarian. Student workers always directed customers to restrooms, but they usually did not attempt to answer other directional questions like "Where are the music CDs?" A stack of one-page library maps was available at the desk, but student staff rarely pointed out locations on the maps. In fact, they sometimes seemed unaware of the maps altogether. Student staff always restricted their answers to the specific questions being asked. They rarely sought clarification or probed to discover the underlying information need. That meant they sometimes answered the wrong questions.

The Role of Student Staff

By the way, I also had an opportunity to lurk at another academic library that was quite similar to the one I've been describing. Several students assisted customers at the circulation desk, while permanent staff members worked at office desks behind a glass partition. It quickly became evident that the heart and soul of this student staff was Jeremy. He was a very loquacious young man and obviously enjoyed presiding over the desk. It always seemed to be Jeremy who answered student questions, but, unlike Tiffany, he viewed them as opportunities to start conversations. In other words, he asked somewhat probing questions, answered directional questions more or less correctly, and sometimes even answered what I would call reference questions. Because I could not hear everything that was said, I tended to notice body language more. Students asking questions responded with smiles, nods, and a firm step as they headed toward the resources recommended by Jeremy. By coincidence, I happened to encounter Jeremy in the elevator. I introduced myself and complimented him on his skill at answering customer questions. "Please don't say that to Mrs. S.

[one of the permanent staff members working behind the glass partition]. She says students aren't supposed to answer so many questions."

I suddenly felt a stab of guilt. Both you and I have known many Jeremys. We complain that we just can't shut them up and they don't know their limits. I am sure I have responded in much the same way as Mrs. S., attempting to restrain a "know-it-all" student or commiserating with a circulation supervisor who was trying to do so. We correctly assumed that a permanent staff member would be able to provide more accurate information than a student worker, but then we left the student on his own. Neither Jeremy nor the other students really understood the definition of a reference question. Either they answered the questions or they didn't. Either they relied on their own knowledge or pushed the customer off on someone else. Tiffany and most other student assistants discovered it was easier and safer to avoid answering questions. In fact, since the library training they had received consisted entirely of computer routines, checkout periods, and overdue fines, their actual knowledge of the library was negligible.

Suddenly, as an outsider, I saw clearly that Jeremy's customers were much better off than Tiffany's. First, they were warmly greeted by a personable young man and felt more at ease in the library. Because there were many more directional questions than reference questions, customers usually saved time and found the service or collection they were looking for. When Jeremy answered a reference question incorrectly, customers probably wasted time before they were finally steered to the reference desk. I imagine, however, that if you surveyed Jeremy's customers as they were leaving the library, they probably had a much more pleasant and successful experience than Tiffany's customers.

Twice while I was nearby, the permanent staff member at Tiffany's library assisted a customer. In one case, the customer had protested an overdue fine and the matter was turned over to the "voice of authority." In the other case, the staff member was passing through the area and overheard the question. What a difference in service! First, the staff member listened, and it suddenly became clear to me that with the exception of Jeremy, student assistants rarely listened to customer queries. That was probably because they depended on two or three all-purpose responses to cover every possible situation. Second, a real conversation took place. Again, I could not hear the entire exchange, but both their faces were animated. The staff member asked questions until she understood the information need and then made several suggestions, using the map as a visual aid. The entire exchange took only a few minutes, but the difference in the customer's response was amazing. He was smiling as he walked rapidly and decisively through the double doors. Unlike Jeremy's customers, he not only felt welcome and more at ease, but he received reliable guidance from a knowledgeable staff member. The likelihood that he would find what he was looking for rose accordingly, as did the chances that he would return to the library again. As I said, however, this kind of exchange happened only once while I was observing.

Customers come into this large and confusing building, see what appears to be a help desk, and expect to be helped. Circulation is the one service desk that all library customers usually pass. After "lurking" for perhaps twenty minutes, it became clear to me that there was really not much point in customers stopping at the desk unless they were returning or checking out library materials. Because this library also had self-checkout stations, it probably wouldn't make much difference to many library customers if the circulation desk disappeared in a puff of smoke.

I do understand that most academic library staffs are stretched thin and student workers are badly needed. Most libraries could not function without their student legions, and it is certainly possible for them to play a more positive role in customer service. However, they can play that role only when and if they are fully trained and carefully supervised. Although I observed a number of personable student workers, it was clear that training and supervision were in short supply. Other students, who were not fortunate enough to obtain on-campus jobs or who sought a different kind of experience, are working part-time in the community. They are serving as administrative assistants, pharmacy clerks, and even bank tellers. They are real employees who must contribute to their employers' profitability. Training and supervision are needed to achieve that goal, so these are usually provided. What makes library student employment different is that they are not considered real jobs with real goals. The "no-man's-land" into which college students receiving student aid are deposited by the library and other campus departments simply does not exist on Main Street.

Academic libraries appear to exhibit what might be described as schizophrenic behavior. The libraries described above (I'll continue to call them "Tiffany's library" and "Jeremy's library," since these students represent the library to so many customers) are dedicated to serving their customers. Their mission statements attest to this goal, and even relatively junior staff members have been told again and again that service is a top priority. At the same time, customer service takes time away from real work and is widely viewed as a frill. It even seems that while more lip service is paid to it, the quantity and quality of customer service may actually have declined in the past twenty years. How can this be so? Let's take a look at some possible causes.

COMPUTERIZATION

The tasks involved in record-keeping once occupied much of the time of most library staff members. Old-timers will remember the hordes of library employees who used to work in cataloging, acquisitions, and technical services departments. Typing each order slip and catalog card occupied a huge amount of time. Each of the five copies of the order slip had a file of its own, and catalog cards had to be works of art. Computers freed libraries from most of that drudgery, but somehow the perfectionism that created those catalog cards transferred itself to computerized records.

If we take a look at one of today's typical automated library systems, we must admit that it would be difficult to do any real damage to the system. Passwords protect critical global settings, backups are usually automatic, and real meltdowns are relatively rare. Making a mess of one transaction will not affect the thousands of others or the integrity of the system. Yet the circulation staff member in Tiffany's library devoted most of her time to computer procedures. I doubt that she would say these tasks were more important than serving customers, but she would definitely consider them more critical to her job security and advancement. To understand why, perhaps we might look in on her annual evaluation conference with her supervisor, the access services manager.

In most academic libraries, staff are evaluated annually. Positive evaluations result in salary raises; poor ones may lead to probation, and so-so evaluations are depressing, making it clear to staff members that they are "going nowhere." Supervisors, of course, find evaluations difficult and stressful. Negative evaluations are likely to be contested, so supervisors tend to limit their criticisms to easily verified problems. Because fairness requires that the same standards be applied to all evaluations, positive evaluations are also based on verifiable information. Unless one is lurking near a service desk as I did, good or bad customer service is difficult to verify. Tiffany and her fellow student assistants had been taught to be polite to customers and to give the appearance of being helpful. Customers may have been somewhat dissatisfied with the answers to their questions, but not usually dissatisfied enough to register formal complaints.

They did, however, complain when they were charged for books they knew they had returned. In other words, most complaints are the result of computer mistakes, and complaints tend to find their way to supervisors. Computer mistakes are also easier to identify. When an error is made on a borrower's record and an overdue notice is returned, many systems make it possible to identify the staff member who created the record. There still exist in today's library culture the ghosts of those long-ago staff members who concerned themselves with the spaces after the period on those archaic catalog cards. In other words, some of their focus on detail has transferred itself to today's staff members, and it is not uncommon for one staff member to complain loudly about another's irregular records. Finally, computers make it easy to know when work is being kept up-to-date. It is easy to discover whether overdue notices have been sent out on time or whether customers have been notified of materials being held for them. In a sense, computers make it easy for a supervisor to figuratively look over staff members' shoulders and see what they have been up to.

It can happen, therefore, that the access services manager in Tiffany's library, meeting with a staff member, has little information on which to base her evaluation except the staffer's success in performing computerized procedures. Perhaps the manager spends most of her time sitting at her own desk, far removed from the hubbub of the public area, checking time sheets, answering e-mail, and attending to a dozen personnel matters that keep her from noticing problems with customer service. Is it any wonder that routine clerical tasks come to be of paramount importance to the circulation staff and customer service seems like a nice extra?

THE CHALLENGE OF MULTITASKING

During the past few years, we have been hearing (and seeing) the words *multitask* and *multitasking* thrown around at library conferences, in-service workshops, and in a wide array of library literature. It is a concept that has found its way to libraries from the business world, especially computer systems management, and it is usually considered a good thing—something that library staff members should spend more time doing. The term is usually defined as doing more than one task or duty at the same time. Computers may be able to do several things simultaneously, but in the case of human beings, multitasking usually means moving from one duty to another in rapid succession. Most studies conclude that typical workplace tasks do not require intense mental concentration and so lend themselves to multitasking. Highly challenging tasks require a greater degree of concentration than multitasking permits, but the cliché "It's not rocket science" is still surprisingly appropriate. Research also indicates that most people can multitask adequately and do so constantly in their personal lives.

Let's take another peek at the circulation staff member who was "on call" in Tiffany's library. In fact, let me repeat her comment. "Tiffany knows that I'm here if she needs me. I have to get my work done, but all she has to do is call. I'm happy to interrupt my work to serve the public." What was the work she was doing that could not be done at the circulation desk? When I visited with circulation staff, I typically found them doing one of the following:

- reading and replying to staff e-mail
- reading electronic discussion list mail
- reviewing student time sheets and related paperwork
- printing and sending out overdue notices
- processing reserve materials
- printing out statistical and other reports generated by the automated library system
- responding to faculty requests or complaints

Although circulation job descriptions were much more extensive, I did not actually see permanent staff performing most of the tasks specified in them. I mention "responding to faculty requests or complaints" separately in the above list because in some libraries, the staff are fearful of faculty complaints. They may respond personally to their requests, fearing that student assistants might provoke criticism. In other libraries (usually larger ones), little distinction is made between faculty and student customers.

If we assume that the circulation staff member spends most of her time performing the tasks listed above, there is really no reason why she couldn't do a sizable number of them at the circulation desk. Most of us read and respond to e-mail almost anytime anywhere. If she performed the majority of the other tasks listed above while making herself available to customers, she should have little difficulty. In fact, tasks like printing and sending out overdue notices could easily be done by student assistants, leaving the staff member more time to assist customers. In other words, she has entrusted students with more demanding responsibilities while she herself performs simpler, more repetitive tasks. Processing reserve materials is another task that can be done by well-trained student assistants, and by spending more time at the desk, the staff member can more easily supervise the process. Although circulation staff members certainly perform a variety of tasks not listed above, personnel matters are often the only tasks on this list best performed away from the desk. Some of the information may be confidential, and loose papers can easily become lost.

COMPARING LIBRARIES TO BOOKSTORES

A key factor in successful customer service is selecting the best applicants for paraprofessional and clerical positions. Several years ago, I was gathering information for a book comparing libraries with large chain bookstores.

I discovered that the duties of a circulation assistant and those of a customer service representative were very similar. Both bear the responsibility of representing the bookstore or library to customers, since they are by far the most visible staff members. Both answer directional and simple reference questions. Both must be able to perform several basic computer routines, and both scan books and other materials to enter them into the computer system. Naturally, library staff handle returned materials much more often than bookstores, and bookstore staff deal with a lot more money.

Both organizations have almost the same pool of applicants available when they have a job opening, because the pay scale and advertised qualifications are similar (although libraries may offer better benefits). Nevertheless, supervisors appeared to weigh these qualifications very differently. Both library and bookstore managers valued intelligent applicants who could perform clerical tasks accurately and efficiently. Bookstore managers, however, selected the applicants who had the most pleasing, outgoing personalities if they also appeared competent. Library managers nearly always chose the applicants whom they thought were best able to get the work done. In job interviews, library supervisors almost always asked if the applicant liked working with people, the applicant always said yes, and that was usually the end of it. Of course, if applicants exhibited signs of difficult or antisocial personalities, they were probably excluded from consideration, but most people are at their best at a job interview.

Work at a public service desk, however, can be extremely tiring for introverts. It is essential that staff working primarily with the public enjoy these contacts with strangers and become energized by them. Customers know when staff members are enjoying their company and when they are being politely tolerated. No matter what helpful services the library provides, no matter how extensive its collection, customers will leave the library with a neutral or negative impression if they don't feel the spark of human kinship. That personal interaction with another human being will usually outweigh other feelings. If staff members really don't enjoy working with customers, they will find excuses to avoid them, and this may be the main reason for the many invisible circulation staff members. In bookstores, it is not usually possible to disappear from view. Introverted staff members are not able to create their own jobs that minimize contact with the public. Both they and their supervisors will soon realize that this is not the job for them, and they will soon move on to other employment. Too often, I'm afraid that they may move on to libraries.

PUBLIC INTERACTION IN REFERENCE SERVICES

Just as circulation assistants may attempt to avoid working with the public, librarians also avoid working at the reference desk. There are, however, some more credible reasons for this avoidance behavior. Reference librarians need access to their computer files and a telephone to perform many of their duties while assisting customers at the reference desk. The file problem is easily dealt with. Most academic libraries operate relatively sophisticated computer networks, and personal files can easily be kept on the network server or copied to the network as needed. What is really needed is a willingness to do so. Typically, librarians make few preparations prior to the start of their shifts on the reference desk. They grab a few library journals and go out to the desk. Because the reference desk tends to be busy at certain times of the day and deserted at others, there are times when librarians have little to do but read book reviews, surf the Internet, and perhaps even twiddle their thumbs. The ability to get into their files would go a long way toward making these downtimes more productive.

The other thing that limits librarians working at the reference desk is the difficulty involved in making and receiving phone calls. Instruction librarians must work with faculty; librarians with supervisory responsibilities need to communicate with staff members. Some reference areas are too noisy for telephone calls, and others are so quiet that we risk disturbing customers with our calls. Talking on the telephone also tends to absorb our attention more than most tasks, and we risk ignoring customers. You know yourself that when you seek help in an office or store, you accept the fact that you must wait your turn if other customers are ahead of you. However, you find yourself becoming annoyed if the service representative continues to talk on the telephone for more than a few minutes.

The Joy of Messaging

One day, I was visiting with a librarian who was working in her cubicle. She was telling me about her library's very successful instruction program when she noticed my eyes had strayed to her computer screen. She immediately flushed and guiltily admitted that she kept the Yahoo! instant messaging program loaded in case her son or her husband wanted to contact her. There was no reason for her guilty reaction, because it was obvious that she wasn't wasting her time chatting when she should be doing her work. Instead, she used the program as an efficient way of staying in touch with her family without interrupting her work for phone calls. It is my impression that the majority of students, faculty, and staff members under the age of forty also find IM useful. Why then can't librarians working at the reference desk do the same? Why can't they share their user names with students who may need assistance, faculty members, and library staff members? If they use IM for both library activities and their personal needs, they may wish to create two user accounts.

If the messaging program were loaded on a computer at the circulation desk, Tiffany might forward a reference question. If the reference desk has its own user name, it can be posted at OPAC stations throughout the library. That would make it possible for students to get reference help wherever they might be studying. The downside of messaging programs is that they pose potential security problems, so some libraries choose not to install them on public computers. However, sound security practices like regularly deleting downloaded files and regularly restoring computer settings make it possible to peacefully coexist with instant messaging.

IM programs are just one way to make it possible for librarians to get most routine work done while assisting customers at the reference desk. Academic libraries are currently experimenting with a variety of virtual communications media, including texting and chatting. Texting has become the hottest innovation among young people, and it works well for them because they can text to or from anywhere using their cell phones. Internet chatting continues to be popular because it provides an opportunity to interact with a large group of people.

Electronic Communication in Real Libraries

Perhaps the best discussion of instant messaging and texting in academic libraries can be found in the July 2007 issue of *Reference Librarian.* In one of the articles, Sarah Steiner and Casey Long discuss the results of a survey they conducted on librarians' attitudes toward instant messaging. Their article, "What Are We Afraid Of? A Survey of Librarian Opinions and Misconceptions Regarding Instant Messenger," covers most of the relevant issues.[1] For example, they report that the Pew Internet and American Life Project found in 2005 that over 42 percent of all online individuals used an IM program. A similar study conducted by America Online found that among younger Internet users, the number rose to 90 percent. Because this latter group constitutes the primary market for academic library services, it is clear that messaging is an effective way to communicate with customers. Steiner and Long point out that today's students expect libraries to be available online. They conduct most of their personal business online and expect libraries to be part of the online world. The study found that approximately 25 percent of the librarians surveyed used instant messaging to communicate with their customers, and in general they have found that IM increased the number of reference questions received.

The authors also compared the use of chat reference to IM. Although at the time the survey was conducted, chat reference was offered at more academic libraries, it appears that IM use is growing faster than chat. Librarians sometimes found chat software "clunky" and difficult to work with. They reported that most of the chat packages were developed by information professionals for information professionals, and students didn't like them. IM offered a simpler interface and a greater degree of privacy, which is important if customers feel embarrassed at their ignorance or need confidential information. On the negative side, librarians expressed concerns about the need to sign up for an IM account. Although most customers already have accounts, signing up can discourage those who must sign up just to ask an online question.

Some libraries offer both chat and messaging, theoretically providing their customers with the best of both worlds. A few librarians, however, especially older ones who found the technology complicated and difficult to manage, thought this was unnecessary and did not result in better service. Others complained about the difficulty in collecting statistics, but this problem does not exist in Trillian and Gaim, two programs frequently used in academic libraries. These have the dual advantages of being able to communicate with all the more popular messaging programs and to maintain transcripts of all sessions. Sessions can be sent and saved to one master computer workstation. In fact, most of the difficulties that once limited IM use in libraries no longer exist. For example, it was once necessary for customers to download client software to use services like Yahoo!, AIM, and MSN. These services now make it possible to use their messengers on the Internet without any special software. IT departments have sometimes opposed messaging because of security problems, but the survey found that most of the feared security breaches never actually occurred. By simply ignoring suspicious links sent by a few malicious customers, librarians were able to avoid most intruders, and their antivirus programs usually caught any other problems.

When Instant Communication Means a Three-Hour Delay

In another article in the same issue of *Reference Librarian*, J. B. Hill and colleagues recount their experiences with the "Text a Librarian" project, which introduced texting to the Sims Memorial Library at Southeastern Louisiana University.[2] Librarians learned that in 2005, approximately nine in ten college students owned cell phones and carried them throughout the day. It therefore seemed that this could be a very effective way to stay in touch with most of the university's students. The library contracted with a vendor in Australia to transform text messages into e-mail messages. Thus, the text messages that customers might send from home or from the fourth floor of the library appeared at the reference desk as incoming e-mail. The program has generally been considered successful, but the number of questions received remains small.

One reason could be that the library's promotional literature and website tell customers that they can expect a response within two or three hours when the library is open. This is, unfortunately, not the way that college-age students use texting. They are accustomed to an immediate response. When customers need reference assistance, they also need it immediately. They have reached a point in their research at which they have become "stuck." They are unable to continue without help. In two or three hours, they will have either wasted a lot of time or they will have moved on to something else. Thus, the most immediate way of accessing the library can also become the slowest.

The whole concept of digital reference may suffer from this same misunderstanding. When customers walk up to the reference desk, they are usually helped almost immediately. True, they may have to wait a few minutes, but they will quickly obtain enough information to continue with their quest. Similarly, when customers phone the reference desk, they usually receive an immediate response. Of course, more complicated questions require a callback, but reference librarians are accustomed to providing immediate assistance to both in-house and telephone customers. Somehow, digital reference, which may mean e-mail, online chat, instant messaging, or texting, is not viewed with the same sense of urgency. In fact, when I checked a number of academic library web pages offering digital reference service, I discovered that some specified a turnaround time of up to three days.

As James Rettig puts it,

> our students expect to be able to receive service any time of day or night, any and every day of the week. They expect [the] service to respond to them as quickly as their logged-on IM buddies respond, even though, as we know, an online reference transaction, including, of course, the reference interview, is inherently more complex than exchanges consisting of . . . spoken language.[3]

Essentially, this means that while librarians are relegating virtual reference to the back burner, fitting it in when their schedules permit, customers are expecting an immediate response. They are accustomed to what amounts to instant communication. To complicate matters further, Rettig points out that everything our profession knows about reference service tells us that it cannot be done well without allocating considerable time and attention to the reference interview. He goes on to say:

> These values implicitly undermine good reference service which, even when delivered in a short time, is far more deliberative than one-line volleys of contraction-packed instant messages . . . Nevertheless, we must recognize that the slogan of the Kash 'n Karry grocery chain, "Fresh, Fast and Friendly," sums up key expectations students have of any service.[4]

Somehow, we must reach out to our customers and learn ways of communicating with them that can satisfy their needs. For most traditional-age students, these methods of communication are an integral part of their lives. They usually spend an hour or more each day talking with friends and family in this way. I use the word *talking* here even though their vocal cords are not involved, because for our customers, these are real conversations. They are little different from and are almost as immediate as face-to-face conversations. When electronic communication is translated into a library environment, however, that sense of a conversation may be lost. A text message usually consists of only a line or two. The friend responds with another few lines, and the conversation continues. How could anyone possibly carry on a conversation, or conduct a reference interview for that matter, with two- or three-hour intermissions between responses?

The Art of E-mail

E-mail is another example of a digital communications medium that is seen very differently by different people. Younger people, whether they are at home or at work, tend to leave their e-mail clients open on their computers. An incoming message is usually accompanied by a tone and an announcement signaling its arrival. Regular e-mail users have become accustomed to responding quickly and clearing the message out of their in-box. In fact, experienced e-mail users know how to minimize spam and keep their in-boxes uncluttered so that they can quickly spot and attend to new messages. Over the course of my many meetings with librarians and other staff members, I have found myself glancing at their computer screens.

It is not uncommon to see hundreds of messages clogging their e-mail programs. How on earth is it possible to communicate efficiently if important messages are lost in a sea of spam and old posts that may or may not have been answered?

Most academic libraries now encourage customers to send their reference questions to a library e-mail account. Based on my own informal surveys, it appears that a response delay of two or three days is not uncommon. Library staff may not respond during the weekend, and in some libraries messages are answered only during normal business hours. In other words, it seems as if academic libraries have added digital reference as a trendy new service but have never equated it with "real" reference service. Imagine a customer waiting at the reference desk for two or three days. Imagine a telephone at the reference desk that goes unanswered for that length of time. One wonders if these libraries realize the anger they are generating in their customers, customers who have come to expect the immediacy offered by electronic communication.

THE CUSTOMER'S POINT OF VIEW

As we develop new services, it is essential that we understand why customers might avail themselves of a service and under what circumstances. Most academic library customers are students, so we must concern ourselves with the way they study, prepare for tests, write papers, and perform other academic tasks. In general, we can assume that if they are not performing these tasks in the library, they are doing so at home or in their dorm rooms. We can also assume that in addition to reading their textbooks, they are probably using a personal computer to write essays, complete homework assignments, and access online journal articles and reserve materials.

It is only reasonable to assume that questions will occur to them as they are working at their computers. For example, they can't get into a database; a search strategy that is successful in one database brings up useless hits in another. An instructor promised that electronic reserve materials would be available last Monday, and they haven't yet appeared. Where can they find online examples of APA style? It is at these moments that students are most interested in digital reference services and most likely to submit questions. Because the library has enthusiastically advertised digital reference service, customers may imagine that librarians can help them with whatever library-related questions they may have, and most of those questions require an immediate response.

The day after tomorrow, they will have taken the test, turned in the homework, and moved on to new assignments. Those reference questions will be ancient history. Students may not even remember the questions when at last they find a message from the library in their in-box, but they will remember that the library failed them.

In other words, the library developed a service that satisfies a nonexistent need. It only provides answers to questions that are not time-sensitive. Most students are undergraduates, and most academic librarians have considerable experience with undergraduates. We know perfectly well that this is not the way they work. Why, therefore, did we devise a service that we knew from the beginning would not meet their needs? Even worse, why would we deliberately set the stage for a negative library experience? The fine print on our websites and printed literature usually includes some caveat about turnaround time, but the whole concept of electronic communication shouts immediacy. What else is "instant" messaging if not instant? What student could possibly imagine that her text message would be sent all the way to Australia, then converted into an e-mail message and sent back to the library, only to sit in the reference department's in-box? Aren't we merely making a show of embracing these new forms of electronic communication without understanding how they are understood by our customers?

STAFFING THE REFERENCE DESK

Moving Back to the Desk

One library that I visited tried a very interesting experiment. This was a college library that served approximately 1,500 students. The eight librarians on the staff were all involved in the reference rotation, although the library director had fewer desk hours than the others. At most times, the desk was staffed by one librarian. For some time, both the library director and the librarians had felt that they were not doing a very good job of providing reference services. Like the circulation staff member discussed earlier, some of the librarians considered their reference shifts a waste of time when they had so much work to do. Others believed that the quality of reference help tended to be poor. Some of their peers, they felt, made no effort to improve their reference skills, and they rarely conducted anything resembling a real reference interview.

The problem came to a head when a faculty member formally complained about the reference help his class had received with a recent project.

This was a perceptive faculty member known and respected by most of the librarians. The complaint was well reasoned and hit home. The library director charged the professional staff with rethinking the whole issue of reference service and coming up with a program that better met the needs of students and faculty. Much soul-searching followed, including admissions by several librarians that they knew very little about reference. It had never really seemed worth the time and effort to upgrade their skills.

In the end, it was decided that two librarians, not one, would staff the desk during most hours. Librarians would also work more evening and weekend hours, although paraprofessionals would help out as well. When possible, more experienced reference librarians would be paired with less experienced ones. In this way, the more experienced ones would serve as mentors or role models. This meant, however, that other duties might suffer. Librarians would have to find ways to do more of their work at the reference desk or they would fall behind. At the very least, this meant they would need a place to keep their stuff—their personal possessions and work-related books, papers, and supplies. They would need to access their files on the reference computers and spread their materials out on the desktop.

It quickly became clear that the tall, custom-built reference desk would have to go. Sitting on high stools for any length of time was uncomfortable, and so librarians usually stood. If their shifts were going to be twice as long or twice as frequent, they must have comfort. Once lower desks replaced the mammoth reference desk, customers had to look down on the librarians, and this wasn't very pleasant for either party. Customers didn't mind standing when they had a quick directional question, but they dragged chairs over for more involved reference questions. The chairs stayed and multiplied. As we all know, when two people are sitting facing one another in comfortable chairs, conversation happens. Questions became discussions, and a lot more information was exchanged. Occasionally, the second librarian would hear something interesting and join the discussion as well.

For a number of years, the library had encouraged customers to make appointments for reference conferences, which usually consisted of half-hour meetings with reference librarians. Although the service was advertised on the library website and in most of its printed literature, few students ever availed themselves of the opportunity. Now that customers were actually talking with librarians, they began to realize how helpful the conferences could be. Discussions that began at the reference desk were continued later when librarians were able to devote their full attention to one person. Once again, the change meant that more time was needed for reference duties and less was available for other responsibilities. More librarians were also attending reference workshops and conferences. The additional time at the reference desk and the mentoring of more experienced librarians made several reluctant librarians realize what limited help they had been providing.

Evolving Job Descriptions

Nevertheless, there was still downtime at the reference desk. There were many times when only one librarian was working with a customer, and there were times when both librarians were able to get their other work done. Gradually, they learned what tasks lent themselves to being performed in a public area and what kind of work required more privacy. In the past, there had been an unspoken rule that the reference desk should remain impersonal and should not be cluttered. This rule had to go, but it took a while to reach a consensus on just how much mess was okay. The kind of individualism offered by a cubicle of one's own was not really possible, but the librarians soon learned that the freedom to make a little mess is essential to a comfortable work environment. There were times when some complained that desks were piled with too much "stuff," but since both librarians and customers were happy with the new system, these complaints were not taken too seriously.

Finding time for other duties, however, posed a more serious problem. Job descriptions had not been revised in a number of years, and it was decided that the time had come for reevaluating priorities and making some major changes. Some of the tasks the librarians had been worrying about were clearly less important than customer service. These tasks were removed from the librarians' job descriptions, reassigned to paraprofessional staff members, or reworded to make it clear they were low in priority. Other responsibilities really were important and continued to be viewed as a high priority. The changes satisfied most of the librarians, but one continued to be highly critical of the new reference program. Her frustration finally came to a head at a librarians' meeting. The group, she said, had butchered her job description. They had devalued the jobs she considered important. She did not enjoy working with the public, and it was not fair that so many of the things she did enjoy were no longer considered important.

The library director negotiated a compromise and relative peace was restored. The problem raised, however, is a very real one in many academic libraries. So many of the tasks that librarians performed twenty years ago have been simplified or eliminated by computers or can now be done by paraprofessional staff. This has meant that additional time is available. Sometimes new responsibilities come naturally as the library grows and evolves. In other cases, librarians have responded by expanding their own job descriptions, continuing to perform unneeded tasks or adding new tasks that interest them. This is possible because unlike those of clerical and paraprofessional staff, librarians' job descriptions tend to be more general in nature.

WHEN CHANGE IS PAINFUL

It is often possible for two librarians with nearly identical job descriptions to play totally different roles in a library. Although librarians are professionals and certainly should have considerable freedom in setting their own goals, everyone who works in a library must be headed in the same general direction. When the library's mission statement is focused on serving users and every job description emphasizes this single overarching obligation, how does it happen that individuals have been able to invent competing responsibilities that they believe take precedence over that primary obligation? When these people actively oppose change and passively sabotage important programs, they can do immeasurable harm to the library. We are torn between loyalty to staff who have given a large part of their lives to the library and our mission to make the library relevant to a twenty-first-century academic community.

It is understandable that twenty- or thirty-year veteran librarians may be having difficulty adjusting to change, but we sometimes find these attitudes in much younger staff as well. Why is it that we hire librarians who would be better suited to yesterday's library than today's? Why do we hire people who do not enjoy working with the public when traditional "behind-the-scenes" jobs are the ones hardest hit by change? I think the time has come when we cannot afford to hire any staff member, whether professional, paraprofessional, or clerical, whom we consider a liability working at a public service desk.

NOTES

1. Sarah Steiner and Casey Long, "What Are We Afraid Of? A Survey of Librarian Opinions and Misconceptions Regarding Instant Messenger," *Reference Librarian* 47, no. 97 (2007): 31–50.
2. J. B. Hill et al., "Text Messaging in an Academic Library: Integrating SMS into Digital Reference," *Reference Librarian* 47, no. 97 (2007): 17–29.
3. James Rettig, "Technology, Cluelessness, Anthropology, and the Memex: The Future of Academic Reference Service," RUSA Forums, www.ala.org/ala/rusa/protools/futureofref/technologycluelessness.cfm.
4. Ibid.

RESOURCES

Harney, J. "The Value of Personalization in Customer Management." *e-doc* 16, no. 2 (March/April 2002): 24–26.

Hernon, P., et al. "Service Quality and Customer Satisfaction: An Assessment and Future Directions." *Journal of Academic Librarianship* 25, no. 1 (January 1999): 9–17.

Moysa, S. "Evaluation of Customer Service Behaviour at the Reference Desk in an Academic Library." *Feliciter* 50, no. 2 (2004): 60–63.

Stratigos, A. "The 'R' Word [Relationships]." *Online* (Weston, CT) 26, no. 1 (January/February 2002): 78–80.

Sutton, Lynn. "Collaborating with Our Patrons: Letting the Users Select." Presentation at the Eleventh National Conference of the Association of College and Research Libraries, Charlotte, NC, April 10–13, 2003. Available at www.ala.org/ala/acrl/acrlevents/lsutton.pdf.

10

EVALUATING OUR PROGRESS

Some years ago, I was asked to serve on something called a retention task force. My academic institution was worried about the large number of undergraduate students who dropped out or transferred to other colleges and universities. A highly paid consultant had been hired to investigate the problem, and our task force was charged with developing a set of recommendations based on his findings.

WHEN STATISTICS GO AWRY

The task force members represented a number of different academic and administrative departments. Taken as a group, we knew quite a lot about our students: their strengths and weaknesses, their likes and dislikes. When we studied the consultant's report, however, we were very surprised at some of his discoveries. His questionnaires and focus groups had yielded wholly unexpected responses from students. The admissions representative wondered if her department needed to reevaluate its recruitment procedures. Student services wondered if they had been trying to meet nonexistent student needs. Faculty questioned their course offerings. As you might imagine, our first meetings were charged with excitement as we speculated about the changes we would recommend.

Sometime around our third or fourth meeting, however, we noticed that the young representative from the tutoring program looked puzzled. His program depended on what is usually called "soft money." In other words, much of his funding came from federal grants. "Every day we collect statistical information for the Feds, and every year we have to answer more questions. I don't know where this guy got his numbers, but I'm sure some of them are wrong." We all stared at the speaker. In our institutional hierarchy, he ranked near the bottom. Was this young upstart daring to question someone whose vita glowed with accomplishments and who had once been a university vice president? Doubtfully, we turned to the tables and charts at the end of the report. Superficially, they looked great. However, some of our committee members had supplied the consultant with data, so they were familiar with at least some of the tables. One number after another was cast into doubt. At last, a professor in the business department volunteered to look more closely at the data, and the young agitator from the tutoring department agreed to help.

The bomb they dropped at our next meeting was truly spectacular. Apparently the consultant, or possibly his secretary or graduate assistant, had crunched the data using a statistical software program like SPSS. Inexperienced with the program, this person had set up several key statistical calculations backward. In other words, positives became negatives and vice versa. No wonder he had produced such amazing discoveries! They were upside down! The neat and impressive tables and charts churned out by the computer had initially been accepted without question. Apparently no one outside our committee had examined the results or wondered why they were so unexpected.

Our Reverence for Statistics

Most of us are not statisticians, but we have been taught to be impressed by the neat columns of numbers they produce. We feel a sort of awe or reverence, as if those tables had been handed down from above like the stone tablets handed down to Moses. I have the feeling that some academic libraries spend seemingly endless hours collecting statistical information, only to have it misused or perhaps not used at all. Of course, much of it is demanded by government agencies, and university administrators also like to see columns of figures. Nevertheless, we are a profession that likes to count things. To become more effective, of course, we must have some way of measuring what we are doing and comparing the result with what we did last year or five years ago. Yet we have a finite amount of time, and there are many measures that are of absolutely no value to us. In other words, they don't impress anyone outside the library, and they don't provide any useful information that reveals our successes and failures.

For a great many years, libraries have been measuring inputs and outputs focusing on physical library resources. It has become clear that such number crunching may provide only a very limited and incomplete picture of the library. Digital resources further complicate our efforts because their measurement requires different definitions, often determined by commercial vendors who cannot agree among themselves. To make data comparable across institutions, it may be necessary to sacrifice the collection of other data that could provide a more accurate picture of one's own library. Of course, such comparisons are necessary, but we mustn't forget that we are evaluating our collections and services in relation to our own customers' needs. It should be the aim of data collection to discover whether the library is progressing toward its customer-driven goals or moving in another direction. In other words, the data we collect should tell us whether we are achieving the outcomes identified in our strategic plans, mission statements, goals, and objectives. Outcome measures should tell us what kind of impact our collections and services are having on our customers.

LibQUAL

One of the most important projects undertaken by university libraries in recent years is LibQUAL, a program developed by the Association of Research Libraries to evaluate customer service. Most of us are familiar with it, and we are also aware that many academic libraries have used it to solicit, understand, and act on their customers' opinions. Central to the program is perhaps the best survey instrument that has ever been designed for academic library use, a web-based survey that has been rigorously tested to establish its validity. Extensive training opportunities have been made available to libraries to help them interpret survey results. LibQUAL is an excellent tool for improving library services, changing organizational culture, and marketing the library to the academic community. It has been enthusiastically received and widely implemented, both nationally and internationally.

For just a moment, we might want to compare LibQUAL to the statistical software package used by the consultant in my story above. In itself, LibQUAL can solve no problems, right no wrongs, improve no customer services. But in the hands of well-trained, committed librarians, it can clarify unknowns, allowing libraries to focus their energies on serious problems. When properly used it can

- foster a culture of excellence in providing library service
- help libraries better understand user perceptions of library service quality
- collect and interpret library user feedback systematically over time
- provide libraries with comparable assessment information from peer institutions
- identify best practices in library service
- enhance library staff members' analytical skills for interpreting and acting on data[1]

The first LibQUAL surveys were administered in 2001, and since then a large number of academic libraries have participated in the program. LibQUAL announced in 2007 that it was on track to collect data from 1,000 institutions. Because the data are centrally analyzed, there is little possibility of foolish errors made by inexperienced number crunchers. As far as the twenty-two survey questions can take them, LibQUAL libraries have identified their strengths and weaknesses as seen from their customers' perspective. If they take full advantage of the workshops and other educational experiences that are available to help them interpret and act on the information, librarians can make significant progress toward the creation of customer-driven libraries.

Does this mean that LibQUAL libraries have been struck by figurative lightning bolts and been transformed into models of customer service? Not quite. There's no question that LibQUAL has been helpful, but survey results must be viewed as a snapshot, a reasonably accurate picture of some customer opinions at one moment in time. Academic libraries, however, are in a state of constant change. They add positions when funds are available and cut them during budget crunches. When they add or eliminate services, they often do so with little input from customers. The "big picture" is helpful, of course, but library changes come one decision at a time. Accurate data about specific library services are essential. To be truly valuable, the data must be able to chart change over time; in other words, it must be longitudinal.

MEASURING VALUE

I was recently rereading Pamela Snelson's article "Communicating the Value of Academic Libraries" in *College and Research Libraries News,* and it set me to musing.[2] Perhaps her most important point is that vast as our literature may be, very little is ever written about the topic of value. In fact, academic librarians themselves spend little time thinking about the value of their own work or the value of their libraries. In essence, Snelson poses this question: what is it that is really valuable about today's academic libraries, and how can we convince leaders in higher education of their value? Value must, therefore, be defined by measures that are important to these decision makers. The problem is that we don't have a clear understanding of how presidents, deans, provosts, and department chairs view the library. With all the statistics that we collect, do we actually ask ourselves whether these particular numbers mean anything at all to "the powers that be"? We are more likely to focus our attention on looking good in comparison to our colleagues in other universities than on influencing our own administrators.

When we request new positions or defend the library against budget cuts, which data advance our argument and which mean little to outsiders? If one were to look at the annual reports that libraries produce and disseminate, one would naturally find a lot of positive information about the library. Successes are highlighted, and more positive statistics are included. Yet it's doubtful that we have deliberately and intentionally focused on the kind of information that really matters to academic decision makers. Without the judicious choice of data, as well as concise and lucid interpretation of it, they are unlikely to be impressed by the library's successes. It is up to the library's leadership to serve as translators, connecting the library's achievements to institutional goals.

Support for Institutional Goals

One obvious institutional value in which the library plays an important role is student learning. How can we measure the impact that the library has on student learning? Because this book concerns itself with brick-and-mortar libraries, we must refine and narrow this question. Do the face-to-face services, programs, and resources we provide to our customers make them more successful students? Do those who make the library part of their regular on-campus experience do better academically than those who never set foot in the library? Do students do better academically if they participate in our workshops, our library literacy classes, or our classroom instructional sessions? Can we develop a research design that can quantify our impact on student learning? If we can do this, we will have a much more effective argument for funding than if we produce even the most extensive statistical tabulations.

So many of our statistics are really intended to make the case that we are busy—that a very large number of people enter our doors and a lot of items are circulated to our customers. Impressive though these numbers may be, they fail to speak to the issue of value. One really can't blame academic leaders for finding them less than inspiring. Again, librarians must become interpreters, able to weave a variety of measures into persuasive evidence of the library's value, its vital role in achieving institutional goals. Nearly all of us became academic librarians because we believed in academic libraries. We still believe that libraries are valuable, and our experience supports this belief. Nevertheless, we must accept the fact that this conviction may not be shared by those who hold the purse strings. Even library-literate administrators may remain unimpressed when we fail to reach out to them, when we fail to explain exactly how our successes help them achieve their goals. It is only when we step outside our separate universe with its assumptions, jargon, and esoteric procedures that we can see the library as they see it.

CAO Survey

In 2006 the Association of College and Research Libraries (ACRL) contracted with the Library Research Center at the University of Illinois at Urbana-Champaign to conduct telephone interviews with the chief academic officers (CAOs) of a number of academic institutions.[3] These administrators were told that the ACRL would like to know what academic librarians should be telling them. Preliminary results strongly indicated that CAOs want more attention placed on measuring quality rather than quantity. They want to see the quality of our services measured by users and outside authorities. Numbers mean little if they don't translate into objective evidence of demand and success in meeting that demand. On the positive side, the CAOs encouraged librarians to be more aggressive in asking for resources, in other words, to do more tooting of their own horns.

Armed with this kind of encouragement, why not get to know your own decision makers better? Learn what really matters to them and how the library can play a role in achieving their goals. How do they as outsiders view the library? What opinions do they have of librarians? Do they see them as relevant and involved with the educational process, or do they see them as anachronisms better suited to colleges and universities of another era? When they think of the library, what image comes to mind? Do they imagine vast stack areas, or do they see students actively involved in learning? Which of their buzzwords can you borrow for future reports? How can the library's achievements be expressed in their terms and in keeping with their vision of a successful academic institution? The relationship between the library and the university administration is in part an adversarial one. It is inevitable that we complain about them, but if our constant refrain is "they don't understand us," it's time we start understanding them.

THE BUSINESS OF HIGHER EDUCATION

Academic librarians may be almost unaware of an attitude change that is occurring in public higher education. The growth of state university systems, as well as publicly funded two- and four-year colleges, has been driven largely by the belief that the state has an obligation to provide access to higher education. In recent years, however, a sea change has occurred. Instead of being viewed as a right like secondary education, higher education is more and more being viewed as a business. Pressure is mounting to make students pay a larger share of the cost of their education. Funding is no longer automatic, and the voters want more accountability. Elected officials and state oversight agencies are calling for more cost-effective management, and that includes quantitative evidence of achievement. The academic library must find ways of measuring its contributions to research, teaching, and the service mission of its parent institution. If the library is to continue to be funded even at current levels, it will need to develop better assessment procedures. Other campus departments and divisions are rapidly learning how they can best survive in this new environment and use it to their advantage. Unless the library masters some of the sophisticated assessment tools used in the business world, it will fall behind in the allocation of institutional resources.

One of the many reasons why it is helpful to use the term *customers* to refer to the academic community is to remind us of this new emphasis on running higher education as a business enterprise. Many of us find this idea repugnant. However, to survive and prosper in the twenty-first century, librarians will probably have to put aside any affection they may feel for the ivory tower library of the past. We know that customers make demands, but we rarely think of *patrons* demanding anything. Instead, the term brings to mind individuals who give rather than receive. You might think of patrons of the arts, for example. Their role is to support the arts, not make demands of them. Customers, on the other hand, demand high-quality facilities, resources, and services. They want a library that is focused on their needs, and they have no intention of going out of their way to meet the library's needs or expectations.

Painting a Picture with Numbers

Perhaps because we are required by outsiders to collect so much data, we may come to see them as meaningless. The columns of numbers we produce may mean only support for a budget request, or numbers we'd prefer that no one see because they don't present our library in a favorable light. It is possible, however, to use numerical data simply to know our customers better. Statistical data can help us understand who we're serving and which of our services are best meeting their needs.

With almost no effort on our part, our online library systems collect huge quantities of statistical information. In fact, reports generated by these online systems are so numerous that we sometimes feel inundated by a mountain of numbers. Because the statistical tables thus generated look so professional, we are tempted to include them in the appendixes of our reports without discussing the issues they raise. Which numbers actually mean something?

Which reveal a disturbing trend that can alert the library to a problem and point it in a more productive direction?

Beginning with a Hypothesis

Because the amount of data available is so intimidating, it can be helpful to first decide what you are looking for. You might begin by making some guesses or hypotheses about what you think is happening in your library and therefore what you will find in the data. For example, if you're putting more staff and more money into a service, you should be getting more out of it. You might hypothesize that your efforts have been rewarded by, let's say, a 10 percent increase in the use of the service. In other words, you're not just making a random guess; you're trying to connect cause with effect. What statistical information generated by your system would confirm or disprove this hypothesis? Try to control the urge to peek at the data until you have developed your hypothesis. Being only human, we all have a bad habit of rationalizing the truth, making our hypotheses fit our data, and revising them when the truth fails to meet our expectations. Just as in other aspects of life, it's best to know the bad news. If a program isn't working, you need to know it. If funds are being wasted, you will want to be the one who makes the discovery.

Let's imagine that your library's circulation is down and you want to know why. Do librarians think there is a correlation between increasing e-book use and declining circulation of printed books? How can you use the data generated by your system to determine whether this is true? Similarly, is there an inverse correlation between the use of in-person reference assistance and the use of digital reference? What about long-range trends? What changes have occurred in your library during the past five years? In what ways have services improved, and where have budget problems caused you to cut back? Remember, don't peek! All of us are constantly making assumptions about our libraries, and now's the time to find out how those assumptions square with reality.

Comparing Libraries

Now you can make some hypotheses about how your library's statistics compare with national trends. Consider your academic community, the curriculum, and the effort you have put into publicizing various services. Would you expect that interlibrary loans are increasing more rapidly, or are they roughly on a par with other libraries? Again, you're doing more than just guessing. You know what budgetary resources you have put into programs, which projects have gotten the most attention, and how staff resources have been allocated. Check the ARL's annual statistical compilations for key measures. In other words, you'll want to establish some baselines by researching national trends. However, it isn't very useful to simply compare your library's numbers with others. What is more important is relative growth or decline. If, nationally, book circulation is declining by a certain percentage, how does this figure compare with your circulation? Still another useful strategy is to compare your own library's input and output. For example, what is the relationship between the number of DVDs purchased and the number of DVDs circulated? (You naturally want to know whether your investment is paying off.) Can you establish a trend over the past five years? Are other academic libraries seeing the same trend?

STATISTICAL VALIDATION

As most of us are aware, there are many ways of gathering information. LibQUAL, for example, has produced a seemingly simple evaluation instrument, but a great deal of work has gone into establishing its validity. There are a number of reasons why statistical validity is needed, but perhaps the most important one is that LibQUAL is intended to allow libraries to compare themselves with their peers. Libraries must have confidence that when they score significantly higher or lower than other libraries, it's not just a fluke. If alarm bells are set off by poor scores, librarians need to know whether the problem deserves immediate attention. Otherwise, the effort would be wasted. Without the intensive labor and standardized procedures that have gone into the LibQUAL project, we could not be confident that libraries were measuring the same thing.

Is Validation Needed?

Sophisticated survey instruments like LibQUAL, though they provide high-quality information, do not really provide very much information. Libraries need to know a lot more about their customers if they are to serve them effectively. We usually make decisions in both our personal and work lives based on the information we collect from our environment. In most cases, this is an informal process. A friend recommends a pediatrician, so we make an appointment for our child. We may look up some information about this physician on the Internet, but we don't conduct a formal survey of his or her patients. If we were choosing a brand of paper towels, we would put less effort into the decision because it is less crucial to our family's well-being. Nevertheless, we live our lives more successfully by collecting and informally evaluating information.

Most experienced librarians have been on some campus committee or task force that decided to administer a survey. After a lot of people spent a great deal of time and effort, the result was often not what they hoped for. While the group expected to use the data they collected to solve a problem, the data were not really conclusive and did not tell them a lot that they did not already know. I have a feeling that the reason for some of this dissatisfaction is that the group members had very different expectations. Some, who possessed strong backgrounds in statistics, focused on establishing the reliability of the information collected. They had been taught to distrust information that could not be analyzed and verified. Other members of the group wanted to ask wide-ranging, thought-provoking questions. In fact, they expected much the same kind of useful feedback they received when they questioned their friends or colleagues. These two expectations are actually poles apart. They require different strategies and evaluation methods, so it is most unlikely that both expectations can be met with the same survey. In the end, it is unlikely that either faction got what it wanted.

Collecting Information from Library Customers

Within the library, we often experience a similar problem. We want to know how our customers feel about the library, but we tend to ask their opinions only when we need ammunition to advance our own plans. That's probably because most forms of information gathering are extremely time-consuming. Libraries can ill afford laborious projects because they are already short-staffed. They tend to wait until they need support for an accreditation visit or a budget request. It is certainly true that a survey showing how much the academic community loves the library can be very helpful. Because we all live in the real world, we must defend our library's interests as best we can. However, when we administer a survey at such a time, we are not really looking for new information, and we may be wording our questions to elicit the most positive results. This means that we may sincerely believe that we know what our customers want when, in reality, we have not asked the right questions.

Information That Isn't Being Gathered

It's a good idea for every academic library to take a good look at the data it is collecting. What is being measured and for what purpose? If data are being collected because someone outside the library is asking for it, it is only fair to ask what the library will get out of the effort. Of course, you must complete government forms, but how much staff time should be allocated to the job? Collecting data for accreditation reports comes closer to home. Accreditation is a major institutional goal and therefore important to the library. Of course, there may be ways to spend less time and collect more useful information, but this is definitely a necessary exercise. Other data are being collected to support the library's requests for additional funding. Just as important as any of these requirements is the library's own need to make decisions based on sound information about its customers. How will the library balance these demands? When can the same data be used on two or more reports? When does the library have a right to decide not to collect certain data because the effort is too great and the payoff is too small? These are important questions that can only be answered if all data collection activities are considered together, not individually as each form arrives or each request comes down from on high.

It may be possible to organize and simplify data collection in such a way that more time is available for collecting information that the library really needs. In other words, the data the library collects for its own use are important and should be given a high priority. However, it need not take as much time as you might think. If a library is collecting data strictly for its own use, in other words, to better serve its customers, I've concluded that simpler is usually better. Perhaps our goal should be to get the most information with the least expenditure of scarce resources. That leads us to the question: what does the library need to know that it does not already know?

How Is the Library Being Used?

Because this book focuses on the library building and the services and resources provided within its walls, it may be very useful to evaluate the way that space is being used. Once again, the focus can be on comparing input and output. What is the cost of maintaining specific areas of the library, and what are the resulting benefits? What staff and monetary resources are being expended on any given library space, and what is the academic community getting out of it? There are probably areas of your library that you haven't really thought about in years. They are remote spots that must be

considered when custodial and maintenance issues arise, but they are usually invisible to most of the library staff. Interior space, however, is one of
the library's most important resources. It is both costly and scarce. Are customers and decision makers getting their money's worth?

Competition for space on most academic campuses is fierce. Almost every department, whether academic or administrative, is seeking to expand
its domain. As programs grow, so grows the need for more space, but new
buildings are often delayed for years and years. Because this is the environment in which the library exists, it's a good idea to look at the library's space
as a department chair, dean, or vice president might. Because some departments on your campus may already have an eye on the library, it's best to
see space usage as they might. I'd like to describe a very successful space
evaluation project that I learned about some years ago. The idea came up at
a librarians' meeting when the group was trying to decide what to do about a
rarely used part of the library building. As the discussion went on, it became
clear that there were other areas that weren't a lot different from this one.
Some library spaces felt like ghost towns while, at the same time, there were
parts of the library that were almost too intensively used.

Evaluating Space Usage

It was decided that the main library could practically be divided into spaces
roughly the size of two classrooms. The dimensions were somewhat flexible because the group didn't want to divide functional areas that were a
little larger or smaller. However, they decided that, in general, the "two-
classroom rule" was necessary to compare "apples with apples." Areas were
mapped out on a library floor plan, a number was assigned to each, and a
librarian was made responsible for evaluating each space. Then, to make
things more exciting, a friendly faculty member was asked to take on the role
of devil's advocate. It was her job to look at the spaces from the perspective of
an outsider, perhaps a department chair who needed more classroom space
or more convenient offices.

The input side of the equation was similar for most spaces. In other
words, the cost of heat, light, custodial services, and maintenance didn't vary
much from one space to another. Of course, more expensive furniture and
equipment, as well as increased electrical and data capacity, drove up the
cost of maintaining the information commons significantly. Staffing costs
were also higher for the commons and the first floor, but these additional
costs were not typical of most of the library. Devising output measures was
more complicated. It was decided that output had to be defined in terms of

value to the library's customers. If customers tended to use an area heavily, the area must have value. It was harder to establish the value of stack areas. If circulation counts for a given area were high, the space had more value for the library's customers. If counts were low, did it mean that the space didn't have value? In noncirculating collections, more frequently used materials had more value, but this was more difficult to measure. Some infrequently used or circulated collections might be justified as a service the library provided to the world of scholarship, but if it was easy to borrow such materials on interlibrary loan, were customers really getting value from the collection?

If an area was infrequently chosen by students as a place to study, if materials were rarely used or circulated, and if the space did not serve any other important and clearly identifiable function, then the cost of providing, maintaining, and staffing it probably outweighed the benefits received. In some cases, it was difficult for the librarians to accept this pronouncement. "But it's kind of a nice place where you can get off by yourself and concentrate." "Sure," responded the faculty member, "it's a nice place if you're a street person who wants to take a nap, but how many students do you see up there? My department could turn it into classrooms, and then we could offer more of our courses at convenient times." "You can't argue that the microform area isn't returning value," argued another librarian. "Think of all those resources compressed into such a small space." "Well, I agree that many of the resources are valuable," countered the devil's advocate, who was now viewed by some as the snake in the grass. "But why do you need to waste all that space on old microfilm equipment? I've never seen more than half a dozen students using the area. All those windows are being wasted, and most of our departmental offices are in the basement. We could partition off that area and house at least six or eight faculty members."

New Uses for Existing Space

Just because a library space is not currently justifying its existence doesn't mean that the space is expendable. In fact, it may be even more beneficial to the academic community than a few new classrooms or offices. Nevertheless, we mustn't let the situation continue. In earlier chapters, we discussed the many twenty-first-century innovations that are being included in academic libraries. How might your own unused spaces return more value for your customers? Take the old computer lab that has been largely replaced by the information commons. It is equipped with plenty of electrical outlets. Would this be a good place for a laptop lounge? If it's located adjacent to the 24-hour study area, could it be integrated into that facility?

The older equipment would pose fewer security concerns, but it may not be worth maintaining. Perhaps the space might better become a snack bar, with vending machines offering food and drink. Another low-use area might be too remote to serve these functions, but it could be just the right place for a great new grad student lounge. On the other hand, turning a large, rarely used space on the top floor into a trendy café might attract new customers. Their route from the library entrance to the third-floor café could be deliberately organized to display enticing resources like popular literature without disturbing customers working in quiet study spaces. Could an enthusiastic advertising campaign make up for the somewhat inaccessible location?

A MATTER OF SURVIVAL

In 2005 OCLC released a report entitled *Perceptions of Libraries and Information Resources* that confirmed the public's stereotypical view of libraries.[4] When they thought of a library, the first thing that came to mind for 69 percent of the people surveyed was "books." Only 12 percent thought of information. Even worse, only 6 percent of college students viewed library resources as better as or more trusted than those found through commercial search engines. In other words, when most students are looking for information, they are looking for information in electronic form and do not think of the library and its books as meeting their needs. While academic librarians view the library as being focused on satisfying their customers' information needs, those very same customers assume that this need is better satisfied elsewhere

Drew Racine, in his article "Bifurcate to Survive!" asks what is to most of us a terrifying question: "How long will it be until the first college president decides that the combination of Google, Google Scholar, and Google Books provides a reasonable trade-off for the millions of dollars spent on campus libraries and decides to eliminate the library altogether?"[5] Academic libraries, of course, must house large collections of books, but that college president is not going to be positively impressed with a library-cum-warehouse, and neither will other decision makers. Remember that each area, each chunk of library space, must be perceived as paying its way. High-density or compact shelving may allow the library to retain more print materials while making a lot more space available to high-use services and resources.

Though there is no point in becoming the librarian's equivalent of Chicken Little, perhaps we should be giving more thought to the library doomsday scenario that Racine describes. Of course, we could sit back and just hope the library's doors remain open, at least until the day we retire. If we choose to do so, however, we will be doing a grave disservice to our customers. Don't they deserve more from us? We know that academic libraries are well worth preserving. If we're going to be faithful both to our customers and to our profession, we will have to make it clear to the entire academic community that the library matters. Armed with a clear understanding of our customers' needs and preferences, there is little question that success is within our grasp.

NOTES

1. Association of Research Libraries, LibQUAL, www.libqual.org.
2. Pamela Snelson, "Communicating the Value of Academic Libraries," *College and Research Libraries News* 67, no. 8 (September 2006): 490–92.
3. Ibid., 491.
4. Cathy De Rosa, *Perceptions of Libraries and Information Resources: A Report to the OCLC Membership; A Companion Piece to Perceptions of Libraries and Information Resources* (Dublin, OH: OCLC Online Computer Library Center, 2005).
5. Drew Racine, "Bifurcate to Survive!" *American Libraries* 37, no. 8 (September 2006): 34–35.

RESOURCES

Cook, Colleen, Fred Heath, Bruce Thompson, and Russel L. Thompson. "The Search for New Measures: The ARL LibQUAL+ Study—A Preliminary Report." *portal: Libraries and the Academy* 1, no. 1 (2001): 103–12.
Hernon, Peter. "Outcomes Are Key but Not the Whole Story." *Journal of Academic Librarianship* 28, nos. 1–2 (2002): 55.
Hernon, Peter, and Robert E. Dugan. *An Action Plan for Outcomes Assessment in Your Library.* Chicago: American Library Association, 2002.
Ikenberry, Stanley. "Higher Ed: Dangers of an Unplanned Future." *State Legislatures* 31, no. 8 (September 2005): 16.
Kane, Thomas J., and Peter R. Orszag. *Funding Restrictions at Public Universities: Effects and Policy Implications.* Washington, DC: Brookings Institution, 2003.
Lombardi, John. "Library Performance Measures That Matter." Presentation at the Library Assessment Conference: Building Effective, Sustainable, Practical Assessment. Charlottesville, VA, September 25, 2006.
Maki, Peggy L. "Developing an Assessment Plan to Learn about Student Learning." *Journal of Academic Librarianship* 28, nos. 1–2 (2002): 8–13.

Mote, C. D., Jr. "The Graceful Decline of Higher Education." *Washington Post,*
    July 4, 2004.
Thompson, Bruce, Colleen Cook, and Russel L. Thompson. "Reliability and
    Structure of LibQUAL+ Scores: Measuring Perceived Library Service
    Quality." *portal: Libraries and the Academy* 2, no. 1 (2002): 1–2.

INDEX

You may also be interested in

Creating the Customer-Driven Library: Also by Jeannette Woodward, this book shares practical lessons for any library's revitalization. Inspired by the success mega bookstores have had by focusing so intently on the customer, this book will give you tips to improve customer service, looks, and functionality in ways that enhance your community mission.

The Academic Library and the Net Gen Student: As students embrace new Web 2.0 technologies like MySpace, YouTube, and RSS feeds, libraries also need to take charge. This book will help academic librarians in public services, technology, and administration to better understand the integral role of technology in the social and academic lives of undergraduates, the Net Generation.

Transforming Library Service through Information Commons: This invaluable guide provides the "how-to" information necessary for institutions considering the development of an information commons. Offering plain-speaking advice on what works, authors Bailey and Tierney provide comprehensive case studies from small and large academic libraries to help librarians implement, provide training for, market, and assess an information commons.

Keeping Current: Keeping up with the ever-growing Web can be an overwhelming challenge for busy librarians. Illustrating ways to overcome the deluge of information, author and librarian Steven Cohen shows how best to utilize current tools. Complete with insightful evaluations of software and products that help librarians do their jobs better, easier, and faster, this practical guide supports reference librarians, as well as subject specialists in public, special, school, and academic libraries.

For more information, please visit www.alastore.ala.org.